Christ *in* You

Living the Christ-life

Christ *in* You

Living the Christ-life

Ralph I. Tilley

LITS Books
P. O. Box 405
Sellersburg, Indiana 47172

ISBN: 9780692021934

LITS Books
P.O. Box 405
Sellersburg, Indiana 47172

Ralph I. Tilley is the executive director of Life in the Spirit Ministries and online
editor of Life in the Spirit Journal. For further information, contact litsjournal.org.

Books available at either . . .

litsjournal.org
amazon.com

*This volume is affectionately and gratefully dedicated to
Paul Mills,
a humble servant of Christ and my former pastor,
who walked to my pew and invited me to give my heart to Christ
in a Sunday evening service, August 1961. The same evening
I was called by God to preach the glorious Gospel, and
traveled to a Bible College to study for the ministry.*

ACKNOWLEDGEMENTS

To Emily and Rochelle (my wife and daughter), who
proofread the entire manuscript;
to Phil Estes and Frances Kinlaw Moore (longtime friends in Christ),
who proofread many of the chapters.
To each of these I am deeply grateful.

Contents

Introduction

While pastoring in Upstate New York in the 1980s, it was a privilege to entertain in our home Scottish evangelist Dr. John S. Logan, who ministered in our church on two separate occasions. Thirty years later, Emily and I hold fond memories of those days, fellowshipping with that godly man, who was mighty in the pulpit and is now with the Lord.

Years ago, Dr. Logan was at a meeting of pastors where Watchman Nee (1903-1972), the saintly Chinese evangelist was present. Logan gave the following account of the impression Nee left upon the ministers.

> After speaking, Watchman Nee was fielding questions from the crowd, and one pastor asked if he could define holiness.
>
> Nee said, "It is the Spirit of Christ in me, plus . . ." and he began to move around the room placing his hands on each pastor in succession and saying, "the Spirit of Christ in you, plus the Spirit of Christ in you, plus the Spirit of Christ in you, plus . . ."
>
> The pastors, Dr. Logan said, were all nodding in consent. Holiness is personal in its reformation of our character into the increasing likeness of the character of Christ, plus it has a definite relational dimension — primarily in how we react and respond to one another.

When Nee had moved all around the room and had arrived back on the platform, the pastors were ready for the next question, but Nee was not finished, yet.

He then proceeded around the room again, saying, "Less the self in me, less the self in you, less the self in you, less the self in you, less the self in you . . ."[1]

God is calling each disciple of the Christ to be increasingly transformed into his Son's likeness (2 Cor. 3:18). It is one thing to be *in* Christ, it is another to *live out* the implications of Christ living in us. The Lord Jesus Christ indwells every believer in the person of the Holy Spirit, and as we grow in the grace and the knowledge of the Lord Jesus, every disciple reflects more and more of Christ and less and less of self — by the power of the Holy Spirit.

The following chapters first appeared as individual articles in *Life in the Spirit* journal over a period of some twenty years. Each chapter addresses some aspect of the Christ-life, and is based on what God in Christ has done *for us* through the salvation events (the atoning death and resurrection of Jesus Christ). The emphasis in this book is primarily about what the Lord Jesus Christ is presently doing *in us,* through the ongoing ministry of the Holy Spirit.

One final note: the poetry at the conclusion of each chapter, unless otherwise indicated, is my own — not actually my own, but something received.

Ralph I. Tilley
Soli Deo Gloria

CHAPTER 1

Christ *in* You

In the fall of 2007, my wife Emily and I traveled to Canterbury, England to attend my graduation exercises. Of the several places I wanted to visit while in England was Westminster Chapel, where the famed Dr. Martyn Lloyd-Jones (1899-1981) ministered for some thirty years.

On the Sunday morning following our stay in Canterbury, we attended a worship service at the Chapel, with four of my family members accompanying us. Before entering the sanctuary, I was struck by the church's signboard, which displayed at the bottom the favorite verse of the deceased pastor: "Christ in you, the hope of glory" (Col. 1:27).[1] Think of it—"Christ *in* you"!

However, before we proceed with this thought, allow me to provide some background. There are five pivotal, historic Christian events which are foundational to the believer's present experience and future existence: the death, resurrection, ascension, exaltation, and the descent of the Holy Spirit.

Christ died. While there are several theories of the atonement which have floated around for centuries, one fact is certain: "Christ died for us" (Rom. 5:8). And as a consequence of his meritorious substitutionary death, believing, repentant sinners are now forgiven and justified freely (see Rom. 3:22-25).

Christ arose. Then there's Easter, the resurrection of Christ. By bringing the Lord Jesus out of the grave to live forevermore, God attested to Christ's veracity—everything Christ testified to while on earth was true. The Father validated his Son's deity—he was indeed the Son of God—and he guaranteed the believer's everlasting security: "He who believes in me will live, even though he dies; . . ." (John 11:25).

Christ ascended. But not only did Christ die and rise for us, he also ascended for us: "While he was blessing them, he left them and was taken up into heaven" (Luke 24:51). These three Christ-events are God's provision for the salvation of all who will believe. These events are both historical and foundational to every other doctrine of the Christian faith.

Christ exalted. But there's more. Why did our glorified Lord ascend into Heaven? The writer of the Epistle of Hebrews states it clearly: "But when this priest had offered for all time one sacrifice for sins, he sat down at the right hand of God, . . ." (Heb. 10:12). And why did our glorified Lord enter Heaven? The writer says, "he entered heaven itself, now to appear for us in God's presence" (Heb. 9:24). And what is Christ doing in God's presence for us? The apostle says he "is at the right hand of God and is also interceding for us" (Rom. 8:34). Christ was *exalted* that he might *intercede* for us.

The Gift of the Spirit

Now for the fifth pivotal, historic God-event. It was on the day of Pentecost that the Father and the Son sent the Holy Spirit, so that Christ—by the Spirit—might indwell every believer: Peter preached: "Exalted to the right hand of God, he [Christ] has received from the Father the promised Holy Spirit and has poured out what you now see and hear" (Acts 2:33). Being deeply convicted for their sins as they listened to Peter's message about the reason for the death of Christ, the hearers cried out: "'Brothers, what shall we do?' Peter replied, 'Repent and be baptized, everyone of you, in the name of Jesus Christ for the forgiveness of your sins. And you will receive the gift of the Holy Spirit'" (Acts 2:37-38).

It is the gift of the Holy Spirit that brings Christ to us — *in* us. The New Testament writers repeatedly affirm this truth about the indwelling of Christ. Here are two examples: "Christ lives *in* me" and "if anyone does not have the Spirit of Christ, he does not belong to Christ. But if Christ is *in* you . . ." (Gal. 2:20; Rom. 8:9-10, emphasis added). Christ *in* you!

Jesus Christ is both a historical as well as contemporary Person. Historical: He died, arose, ascended, and exalted to serve as our Mediator. But inasmuch as he is also "the Living One" (Rev. 1:18), he desires to be vitally and dynamically present in the life of every believer: he is present in his glorified body at the Father's right hand, where he sits as our Mediator. Christ is present in every Christian by his indwelling in the person of the Holy Spirit.

Christ *in* You!

The apostle to the Gentiles wrote to the Colossian believers, "God has chosen to make known among the Gentiles the glorious riches of this mystery, which is Christ *in* you, the hope of glory" (Col. 1:27, emphasis added).

Paul's use of the term "mystery" suggests that this truth of the indwelling Christ was hidden from all except by revelation. Unlike many of the pagan religions of Paul's day, which taught that only an exclusive group could know the secret information of their cultic belief system, the apostle declares to these first-century Christians that the truth of the indwelling Christ is a glorious revealed fact for every true believer — Christ *in* you!

Do we believe this — really believe this? Do we actually believe that this same Jesus — the crucified, risen, ascended Lord — is in reality inhabiting every believer at this very moment?

The Lack

I don't think so. I don't think we believe this because of a glaring failure on the part of many Christians — the failure to believe in a present, contemporary Christ: "Jesus Christ is the same yesterday and *today* and forever" (Heb. 13:8, emphasis added).

Oh, we believe in a historical Jesus — the Jesus who died, arose and ascended. But we don't believe in, or experience, the dynamic

3

reality of "the Living One" — living and reigning in us — in *me*!

Why do I say this?

How can a Christian affirm the truth of the indwelling Christ while he *habitually sins*? How can a Christian affirm the truth of the indwelling Christ while he has no overflowing supply and manifestation of *joy*? How can a Christian affirm the truth of the indwelling Christ while he has no pull to the *place of prayer* when the people of God gather? How can a Christian affirm the truth of the indwelling Christ when his heart is not *broken* over the world's sin and the Church's lukewarmness? How can a Christian affirm the truth of the indwelling Christ when he doesn't regularly get alone with Christ and *meditate* upon his words? How can a Christian affirm the truth of the indwelling Christ when he is *careless* about obeying the commands of Christ?

When our Lord walked among men on this earth, he lived a life of victory, joy, prayer, and communion with his Father, wept over the world and Church, and always did those things that pleased the Father.

While I'm not suggesting that the Christian, as long as he is in this world, will ever perfectly attain to the likeness of Christ, I am persuaded that the average twentieth-century Christian is seriously defective and living far beneath his and her privileges in Christ.

Why are so many Christians not experiencing a life of *victory* in their private and personal lives? Why are so many Christians living life without a continual supply of Holy Spirit *joy*? Why do so many Christians not love the place of *prayer*, live without a *broken heart*, fail to *meditate* on the words of Christ and *fail* in striving to keep his commands?

The Answer

God has the answer. God's answer is Pentecost—the personal invasion of the Holy Spirit inhabiting the believer.

Now let's not get sidetracked here by the phenomena which attended the first Pentecost. Let's go to the *substance* of what happened *in* the hearts of those seeking, thirsting disciples on that day. For whatever conclusions one may reach as to what occurred on that remarkable day, it must include this: it was a *substantive*, life-changing

4

experience for those 120 disciples of the ascended Lord. Pentecost made a difference!

No one can study the life of Peter without being struck by the change that took place in this man—after the Pentecost event. I say this reverently, but it must be said: Though Simon Peter walked with Christ as one of his apostles for three years, he did not become mighty in word and deed until after Pentecost. The fact that Christ died did not produce the Peter that we see following Pentecost. The fact that Christ arose and ascended to the right hand of the Father to intercede for his Church, did not in themselves produce the Peter that we see after Pentecost.

Before Pentecost, Peter lacked spiritual stability and Christ-centered focus; he was weighted down with divided loyalties and uncleansed motives; he feared the faces of Christ's enemies more than he feared God. When depressed, Peter was drawn back to the things he had left; his sectarian spirit drew a narrow circle around his own kind, and his impetuosity and tempestuousness were prompted by an apparent egocentricity. On one occasion, his remonstrance with Christ found its source in Satan himself. And, then, while he said he was willing to die for Jesus, he had yet to fall as grain into the ground and die to the *self* life.

Is it any wonder that the Lord Jesus charged his disciples after his resurrection: "I am going to send you what my Father has promised; but stay in the city until you have been clothed with power from on high" (Luke 24:49). Again, Jesus confided to his disciples before he left them: "If anyone loves me, he will obey my teaching. My Father will love him, and we will come to him and make our home with him" (John 14:23). When was this promise fulfilled? At Pentecost. For on that day Christ (and the Father) took up residence in the hearts of his believing, surrendered followers. At Pentecost the 120 experienced the indwelling fullness and dynamic reality of a Christ *in* them as they never had before.

Whatever one may conjecture about the dispensational factors involved at Pentecost, we do know that something happened that day both *to* and *in* Christ's totally surrendered disciples. There was the descent of the Holy Spirit *upon* them, and a revelation of the Son *within* them. They were baptized with and filled with the Holy Spirit, just as John the Baptist and Jesus had foretold.

The Apostle Paul

What the 120 experienced on that life-transforming day was not unlike what Saul of Tarsus experienced a year or two later. Following his dramatic encounter with Christ on the Damascus Road, he was led by the Spirit to the home of a devout disciple by the name of Ananias. In that home we observe a touching, powerful scene: "Placing his hands on Saul, [Ananias] said, 'Brother Saul, the Lord, who appeared to you on the road as you were coming here — has sent me so that you may see again and be filled with the Holy Spirit'" (Acts 9:17). In this Acts 9 narrative, we read where Paul saw Christ, trusted in Christ, and was filled with the Spirit.

I am persuaded that Paul, in writing to the Galatian Christians over twenty years later, was making reference to this "Ananias Home" experience, when he wrote, "God . . . was pleased to reveal his Son *in* me . . ." (Gal. 1:16). On the Damascus Road Paul had a revelation of the risen, glorified Lord, but it was after he arrived at the home of Ananias that he had a second revelation — a revelation of the Son *within*! And what a glorious inner revelation this was!

The Church's Great Need

Oh, that the entire church of the Lord Jesus Christ would acknowledge and experience this. Oh, that all of the ministers of the Lord Jesus Christ would fall on their faces until they experienced the revelation of the Son *within*.

Whenever I think on these things, my mind invariably recalls a book that ought to be on every pastor's shelf — *The Way to Pentecost*, written by the saintly Methodist, Samuel Chadwick (1860-1932).

As a young English pastor, Chadwick became so *dissatisfied* — that's the key — with his lack of spiritual reality and authenticity, his lack of passion for Christ, his lack of power in the pulpit, his lack of love for people, his lack of quality fruitfulness. He took drastic action. He burned all of his sermons and set out to seek the Lord of the Church to satisfy his thirsty heart.

And as he always does, Christ satisfied this young pastor's heart. In writing about this many years later, Chadwick says, "Pentecost transforms. . . . The commonest bush ablaze with the presence of God becomes a miracle of glory."[2] This is so, because by experiencing a personal Pentecost the surrendered heart has experienced a revelation of the Son within. For you see, Pentecost makes Christ real — alive — alive and real within.

The late Dr. R.W. Dale, pastor for thirty-six years at Carrs Lane Chapel, Birmingham, England, testified to the reality of this experience. One day while sitting at his desk writing an Easter sermon, suddenly the Holy Spirit made the "Living One" real to this hungry pastor. "Christ is alive! Alive! Alive! Can that really be true? Living as I am?"

In recording this event in Dale's life, Dr. Joe Brice writes, "At first it seemed strange, but at last the truth dawned in a burst of glory. The preacher rose and paced about his study repeating 'Christ is living! Christ is living! Yes, Christ is living!' Dale said that this experience had the nature of a new discovery. "I thought that all along I believed it, but not until that moment did I feel sure about it." Then Dale exclaimed, "All my people shall know it. I shall preach it again and again until they believe it as I do now."[3]

What Dr. Dale experienced on that momentous occasion was not unlike what Paul experienced in the home of Ananias, or what the disciples experienced on the day of Pentecost, or what a myriad of other thirsty-hearted believers have experienced. In the words of the late Catherine Marshall, they have experienced "something more." And that *something more* is more than something to be experienced — he is *Someone*. He is the Son, the Lord of glory.

It is one thing to be *in* Christ; it is quite another thing for *Christ* to be *in* you — in all of his dynamic, living reality. Are you thirsty?

Oh, that I may know more than Christ for me!
Oh, that I may know more than I am in Christ!
Oh, that I may have the full assurance
Of Christ in me — a present reality!

CHAPTER 2

Grace and Salvation
(Part 1)

It was 1983. At the time, John Abbott was a hard-nosed regional manager with Thornton Oil Co., living in New Albany, Indiana.

John grew up in a church parsonage and eventually enrolled in a Bible college, from which he was expelled for a minor infraction. John then joined the United States Air Force, serving his country for over nine years. While in the military, he married and divorced. He later remarried, but in time serious strains occurred in that marriage. Finally, his lovely wife LeAnn, a committed Christian, issued an ultimatum: "John, either you get your act together and start going to church with me and the kids or this marriage may end."

John was cornered. He loved his wife and kids and didn't want to lose them. He had to make a choice. And so with great reluctance, he went to both Sunday school and the worship service the following Sunday.

It happened to be a communion Sunday that day at Wesley Chapel United Methodist Church in New Albany. John had decided that he was going to surrender his life to the Lord Jesus Christ when the invitation was given at the end of the service. But when he glanced at the church bulletin he noticed there was no invitation printed.

John then told the Lord that it was *his* problem. In other words, if there's no invitation for sinners to go forward and accept Christ as their Savior, then he couldn't do it—at least not that day, so he thought.

Because of large attendance in their services, usually communion was served to believers in the pews at Wesley Chapel. However, that Sunday, Pastor John Thrasher—a strong evangelical minister—invited the Christians and repentant sinners to receive communion at the altar. John Abbott decided this was his moment. He walked the aisle, knelt at the altar, and promptly prayed: "God, I don't know how to pray. I messed up; you can have me." Whereupon he took the bread and the cup and returned to his seat.

Sitting in his seat, the words of 1 John 3:9 came to his mind, "If we confess our sins, he is faithful and just to forgive us our sins . . ."[1] He was immediately awash with God's peace. He left church that day a new man.

Days later, John walked out of his company's office and witnessed a horrific automobile accident. The accident victim was outside his car and convulsing. A television news crew happened on the scene. John had a strong sense that he should go pray for the man. Then he thought, *How will this look—me, John Abbott—right next to our headquarters, praying for someone.* But rejecting that thought, he hurried toward the man, knelt at his side, and cradled the man's head in his hands and prayed: "Lord, stop these convulsions and give this man peace until the ambulance arrives." Immediately, the convulsions stopped, the ambulance came, and John started walking away.

The news reporter stopped John and said, "I've never seen anything like that before." I'm sure John thought, *I've never done anything like that before.*

Later John was called by the Lord to vocational ministry. He graduated from Asbury Theological Seminary, in time earned a doctor of ministry degree, pastored three United Methodist churches, and for the past several years, Dr. John D. Abbott, Jr. has served on our ministry's board.[1]

Now I have a question: Tell me, how did this radical change occur in this man's life? How? The Spirit-inspired Word of God holds the answer.

A Message of Change
One cannot read the twenty-seven books which comprise our

New Testament Scriptures without noticing that inherent in every conversion to the Lord Jesus Christ is a changed life — changed immediately and definitely at the point of conversion, and continuing to change following the crisis of repentance and saving faith in Jesus Christ.

When the centuries-long prophesied forerunner of the Messiah, John the Baptist, commenced his wilderness ministry, his Spirit-born message was a message of change: "repent and believe in the gospel" (Mark 1:15). After John's imprisonment, Jesus began his mission and ministry with the same message — the message of change: "Repent, for the kingdom of heaven is at hand" (Matt. 4:17). Repentance means change — a radical change of mind, which results in a radical change of conduct.

The Old Testament prophets knew this. John the Baptist knew this. The Lord Jesus Christ — the Word become flesh — knew this. And each of the Apostles knew this, including the Apostle Paul.

He who was once a fire-breathing persecutor of this new Christian sect, following a sudden, dramatic personal encounter with the crucified, risen, and ascended Savior of mankind, became a changed person himself and thereafter became a powerful agent and messenger of change, preaching until his final breath, Jesus Christ — the life-Changer, the Savior.

Titus and Crete

In the course of time, the Apostle Paul was led by the Spirit of God to pen thirteen letters of the twenty-seven books of the New Testament. These letters were written to churches as well as individuals. Those written to individuals consist of four letters, one of which is Paul's *Letter to Titus* — the spiritual overseer of the Mediterranean island of Crete.

While at Crete, as he did on all of his mission travels, Paul was enabled by the Lord to establish churches. But in due course, Paul left the island and purposely left Titus behind to carry on the great work. Later he writes to Titus, reminding him why he left him in Crete: "that you might . . . . appoint elders in every town as I directed you" (1:5). He then proceeded to lay down the spiritual qualifications for elders, warned Titus how to deal with false teachers and teaching, and then informed him what he should teach to older men and women and young women and young men and slaves.

After identifying many of the virtues which are to characterize Christian leaders and all believers, Paul uses the little transitional preposition "for," indicating that all he wrote before, he is now about to tell Titus and us—by the same Holy Spirit who inspired these words—the *purpose* of why he wrote what he wrote.

The Grace of God

"For the grace of God has appeared . . ." (2:11).

The grace of God has been at work in God's creation from the beginning of time. It was present when Adam and Eve fell in Eden's Garden and continued through the preaching of the last of the Old Testament prophets. However, it was the incarnation of the Lord Jesus Christ that was (and is) the ultimate revelation of the grace of God—God manifesting himself in human flesh. The writer of Hebrews sums it up beautifully.

> Long ago, at many times and in many ways, God spoke to our fathers by the prophets, 2but in these last days he has spoken to us by his Son, whom he appointed the heir of all things, through whom also he created the world. 3He is the radiance of the glory of God and the exact imprint of his nature, and he upholds the universe by the word of his power. After making purification for sins, he sat down at the right hand of the Majesty on high, 4having become as much superior to angels as the name he has inherited is more excellent than theirs. (Heb. 1:1-4)

The incarnation of Jesus Christ was the visible, manifest appearance of God's grace—"the Word became flesh and dwelt among us . . ." (John 1:14). From his birth in Bethlehem's manger, throughout his earthly ministry, to his atoning sacrifice, resurrection and ascension—it was the grace of God working in and through the Word made flesh. The apostle wrote: "For the grace of God has appeared . . ." The *grace* of God!

"For the grace of God has appeared, bringing salvation for all people, . . ." (2:11).

The revelation of God's Son, the Lord Jesus Christ, was the perfect revelation and demonstration of God's attitude toward fallen, wayward, twisted, lost sinners — which takes in the entire human race from the beginning of time to the end of time. It is called *grace* because we are undeserving. It is called *grace* because we have no merit. It is called grace because in the words of the prophet, "All we like sheep have gone astray; we have turned everyone to his own way; and the LORD has laid on him the iniquity of us all" (Isa. 53:6). Your iniquity; my iniquity — "the iniquity of us all."

Is it any wonder the first time John the Baptist laid eyes upon the Lord Jesus that he cried out, "Behold, the Lamb of God who takes away the sin of the world!" (John. 1:29)? For in Christ, the promised Messiah, John saw God's very personification, God's very embodiment of grace. Here was the Lamb — the holy, undefiled, spotless Lamb of God. Here was God bringing redemptive solution for all mankind. Jesus himself was the grace of God "bringing salvation for all people" — on that Cross and out from the Empty Tomb.

Shortly following his conversion, an Anglican ordained minister by the name of Charles Wesley (1707-1788), who eventually penned over 6500 hymns, did his best to express with words on paper his amazement and wonderment at the manifest grace of God in bringing salvation through his Son, the Lord Jesus Christ. Here are the first three stanzas of this classic Christian hymn:

And can it be that I should gain
An interest in the Savior's blood?
Died He for me, who caused His pain —
For me, who Him to death pursued?
Amazing love! How can it be,
That Thou, my God, shouldst die for me?

'Tis mystery all: th' Immortal dies:
Who can explore His strange design?
In vain the firstborn seraph tries
To sound the depths of love divine.
'Tis mercy all! Let earth adore,

Let angel minds inquire no more.

He left His Father's throne above
So free, so infinite His grace —
Emptied Himself of all but love,
And bled for Adam's helpless race:
Tis mercy all, immense and free,
For O my God, it found out me![3]

Grace Up Close

Now I want us to turn to an additional passage in the Titus Letter that addresses this matter of salvation and grace from a slightly different perspective. The first passage we looked at identified grace from a more or less historical perspective — that is, God's grace appearing in the person of the Lord Jesus Christ some two thousand years ago, which resulted in his making an atoning sacrifice for man's salvation and redemption. But in Titus 3:4-7, this subject of grace moves from the historical and objective to the personal and experiential.

"But when the goodness and loving kindness of God our Savior appeared, [5]he saved us" (3:4-5).

The "goodness and loving kindness" of God was on full display in the incarnation, atoning sacrifice, and resurrection of the Lord Jesus Christ. If you ask whether or not God is good, look to Bethlehem, look to Calvary, look to the Empty Tomb! God demonstrated his goodness in the provision he made for our salvation; but wonder of wonders! God demonstrates his goodness when he receives us one by one as we are enabled to appropriate his salvation by faith — personally and experientially. Oh, the goodness and loving kindness of God! Who can fathom it? Who can comprehend it?

A.W. Tozer (1897-1963), who made it his lifelong pursuit to know God, to walk with God, said of God's goodness and loving kindness:

The goodness of God is that which disposes Him to be kind, cordial, benevolent, and full of good will toward men. He is tenderhearted and of quick sympathy, and His unfailing attitude toward all moral beings is open, frank, and friendly. By His nature He is inclined to bestow blessedness and He takes holy pleasure in the happiness of His people. . . . Divine goodness, as one of God's attributes, is self-caused, infinite, perfect, and eternal. Since God is immutable He never varies in the intensity of His loving-kindness. He has never been kinder than He now is, nor will He ever be less kind.[4]

Is it any wonder, upon contemplating the goodness and loving kindness of God revealed in the Lord Jesus, that a little twelfth century French monk, Bernard of Clairvaux (1090-1153), wrote,

O hope of every contrite heart,
O joy of all the meek,
*To those who fall, how **kind** Thou art!*
*How **good** to those who seek!*[5]

Paul wrote, "But when the goodness and loving kindness of God our Savior appeared, [5]he saved us" (3:4-5). Six times in this little epistle, the apostle refers to God and the Lord Jesus Christ as "Savior."

1:3 ". . . at the proper time he [God] manifested in his word through the preaching with which I have been entrusted by the command of **God our Savior;** . . ."

1:4 "Grace and peace from God the Father and **Christ Jesus our Savior.**"

2:10 ". . . but showing all good faith, so that in everything they [slaves] may adorn the doctrine of **God our Savior.**

2:13 ". . . waiting for our blessed hope, the appearing of the glory of our great God and **Savior Jesus Christ,** . . ."

3:4 "But when the goodness and loving kindness of **God our Savior** appeared . . ."

3:6 ". . . whom he [the Holy Spirit] poured out on us richly through **Jesus Christ our Savior,** . . ."

God our Savior! Christ Jesus our Savior!

"But when the goodness and loving kindness of God our Savior appeared, ⁵he saved us" (3:4-5).

He saved us! Saved us from *what*?

Christians don't talk much about being *saved* anymore, do they? I wonder why. We say we "went forward." We say we made a "decision" for Christ. We say we were "baptized." We say we were "confirmed." We say we joined the "church." We talk about accepting Jesus as our "Savior." But "Savior" from what?

The angel's announcement to Joseph was, "you shall call his name Jesus" (Matt. 1:21). Jesus (*Yeshua*), means "the LORD'S salvation," or, "salvation from the LORD."

But what is the person who repents of his sins and puts his trust in the Lord Jesus Christ as their Savior saved from? God's Word teaches us that the genuine believer is saved essentially and fundamentally from two things:

The future judgment and wrath of God. "Since, therefore, we have now been justified by his blood, much more shall we be saved by him from the wrath of God" (Rom. 5:9). Again, "For God has not destined us for wrath, but to obtain salvation through our Lord Jesus Christ . . . " (1 Thess. 5:9).

Our sins. Of the scores of occurrences of the word "save" (and its cognates) in both the Old and New Testaments, and of the scores of occurrences of the word "salvation" — they have reference primarily to God through Christ *saving* the repentant sinner from his and her *sins*. The angel said to Joseph, "you will call his name Jesus, for he will save his people from their sins" (Matt. 1:21).

Paul wrote to Titus, "But when the goodness and loving kindness of God our Savior appeared, ⁵he saved us . . ." (3:4-5). Now we can't be saved from our sins without Christ's atoning sacrifice for sins and his resurrection from the grave. But here Paul is addressing personal salvation, experiential salvation — appropriating for ourselves what God accomplished in Christ two thousand years ago.

He saved us! Saved us from what? What was it we needed to be saved from? Our sins! ". . . you will call his name Jesus, for he will save his people from their sins" (Matt. 1:21).

I hear some one say, "I thought I was only *forgiven* of my sins when I repented and trusted in Christ." Oh, you were forgiven, to be sure. Thank God, you were! But what did you repent of—if indeed you did experience genuine repentance? Your sins, right? What is repentance? It's a gift from God which enables us to *turn away* from our sins and *turn toward* God. That is the way Paul put it when reminding the Thessalonian Christians the change wrought in them when they received the word of God under his preaching: "you turned to God from idols to serve the living and true God, . . ." (1 Thess. 1:9).

Are you saved? What did God save you *from*? What evil habits were you bound by? What chains fell off when God saved you?

Though having a godly Christian father and mother; though attending a Church of England chapel from the day of his infant baptism; though a graduate of Oxford University, where among other subjects he studied theology; though he could read the sacred Scriptures in their original languages; though ordained to be a Christian minister; though having spent a few years in the United States in the state of Georgia as a missionary—it wasn't until thirty-one years of age, while reading Martin Luther's commentary on Galatians, that Charles Wesley saw himself as a sinner and trusted at that moment in God through Christ to save him. In writing later of that experience, he wrote,

> *Long my imprisoned spirit lay,*
> *Fast bound in sin and nature's night;*
> *Thine eye diffused a quickening ray —*
> *I woke, the dungeon flamed with light;*
> *My chains fell off, my heart was free,*
> *I rose, went forth, and followed Thee.*[6]

"My chains fell off"!

Are you saved, dear reader? Have your *chains* fallen off? Oh, I don't mean to imply that at the conversion moment, the salvation moment, that all of sin's remnants are gone. God has a lot of work to do in us for as long as we are in this world (God's grace not only saves us, it is "training us" for a lifetime; see Titus 2:11). However, at the conversion event, at the moment we personally experienced God's glorious saving grace—he saved us from our sins and the Holy Spirit entered our lives and we became his sacred temple. From that moment we have a radical and fundamental attitude change toward sin and sinning.

How else can you explain Saul of Tarsus—the Christ-hater and Christian persecutor, becoming Paul the Apostle—the gentle, thoughtful, courageous evangelist, and servant of the Lord Jesus Christ? How else can you explain the change that occurred in him other than his experiencing God's saving grace from sin. How else can you explain a former hard-nosed executive kneeling beside an accident victim, offering a prayer for God to spare his life, who days before would have looked the other way?

The only explanation is the appearance of the grace of God through the Lord Jesus Christ, saving and changing repentant sinners. Such changes can't be accounted for as a mere exertion of the will. The explanation is *grace*—God's grace infusing his divine love into our heart, giving us a clean conscience and a new heart and new life, in order that we might walk in newness of life.

To be saved from the future coming wrath of God is wonderful fact and assurance for the Christian. To be saved—delivered from our sins—in this present age by a good and kind God is no less wonderful and amazing.

Because of Your goodness, love, and mercy,
O God, salvation has appeared for all.
His name shall be called "Jesus," Your spotless Lamb,
Saving each who responds to Your gracious call.

CHAPTER 3

Grace and Salvation
(Part 2)

We observed from the Apostle Paul's *Letter to Titus* in the previous chapter, that God's gracious salvation for mankind is both historical and objective, and personal and experiential.

Titus 2:11 reads, "For the grace of God has appeared, bringing salvation for all people . . ."[1] God's infinite, incomprehensible grace appeared in the incarnation, atoning death, and resurrection of the Word made flesh—the Lord Jesus Christ. This reminds us of a word that never grows old: "For God so loved the world, that he gave his only Son . . ." (John 3:16). This appearance of God's grace-filled action occurred some two thousand years ago in space, time, and history.

Furthermore, we noted that in God's multifaceted graciousness that he desires all people to experience the salvation gift personally and experientially. Again Paul says to Titus, who at the time was the spiritual overseer in Crete: "But when the goodness and loving kindness of God our Savior appeared, he saved us . . ." (3:4-5). While the incarnation, death, and resurrection of Jesus Christ were historical in nature, here the apostle speaks of appropriating God's gift of salvation—"he saved us."

Who could ever forget the day of his or her spiritual birth? While that experience may be as varied as are the stars in the sky; while it may come as a sudden bolt of lightning for some and as a gentle sunrise for others; while for young children the salvation event may not be as pronounced and observable as it is in a forty-year-old adult, nevertheless, for all Christian converts there was a time in which we were dead in trespasses and in sins and a time when we were made alive in Christ Jesus our Lord.

British author C. S. Lewis (1898-1963), who at the time was an atheist teaching philosophy and English at Oxford, likened his conversion to a melting snowman and a person awaking after a long sleep. He writes: "I unbuckled my armor and the snowman started to melt . . ." Then he says, one day "I was driven to Whipsnade [Zoo, London] one sunny morning. When we set out I did not believe that Jesus Christ is the Son of God, and when we reached the zoo I did. Yet I had not exactly spent the journey in thought. Nor in great emotion. . . . It was more like when man, after long sleep, still lying motionless in bed, becomes aware that he is now awake."[2]

One's emotional and psychological experiences are incidental to the conversion event. The substance of what occurred is what is all-important: forgiveness, regeneration, adoption, sanctification (in the sense of being set apart to God) . . . saved from sin!

Now, let us proceed further on this subject of grace and salvation from Paul's *Letter to Titus*.

Righteous Works

". . . he saved us, not because of works done by us in righteousness . . ." (3:5).

Fallen, sinful man has a problem: He thinks he can save himself; therefore he is forever hiding behind the mask of his own *self-righteousness*. The unbeliever, the sinner, believes in his own disillusioned goodness, niceness, and morality.

What was Adam and Eve's instinctive reaction following their dreadful fall? To hide and make for themselves a covering for their nakedness, shame, and guilt. Sin has always worked that way. It compels us to hide—behind false goodness, self-righteousness, niceness, morality, a manufactured belief system.

To quote C. S. Lewis again from his classic volume *Mere Christianity*, Lewis says, "'Niceness'—wholesome, integrated personality—is an excellent thing. We must try by every medical, educational, economic, and political means in our power, to produce a nice world where as many people as possible grow up 'nice' . . . But we must not suppose that even if we succeeded in making everyone nice we should have saved their souls." Then Lewis drives his point home: "A world of nice people, content in their own niceness, looking no further, turned away from God, would be just as desperately in need of salvation as a miserable world — and might even be more difficult to save."[3]

While the Lord has demanded, from the creation of man through the giving of the Law until the present time, his people to live according to his commands and precepts — his people have continually fallen into the snare of self-righteousness. Man without God attempts to *achieve* a righteous life apart from God's gift of righteousness in Christ Jesus the Righteous One.

Saul of Tarsus is a primary case in point (read his testimony in Philippians 2:4-6). Read again the account of the self-righteous Pharisee in Luke 18:9-14. Read what Paul writes of the unbelieving Jews of his own day: "I bear them witness that they have a zeal for God, but not according to knowledge. For being ignorant of the righteousness that comes from God, and seeking to establish their own, they did not submit to God's righteousness" (Rom. 10:2-3).

The late Dr. D. James Kennedy (1930-2007), longtime pastor of Coral Ridge Presbyterian Church in Fort Lauderdale, Florida, tells how our gracious and merciful God stepped into his life and stripped him of his cloak of self-righteousness.

While employed in 1953 as an Arthur Murray dance studio instructor on Florida's east coast, Kennedy was awakened one Sunday morning by his radio alarm clock. The station happened to be tuned to the radio broadcast of Philadelphia's 10th Presbyterian Church, with long-time Pastor Dr. Donald Gray Barnhouse preaching. The first words Kennedy heard from the preacher were in the form of a question: "Young man, if you were to die tonight and stand before Almighty God and he were to say to you, 'What right do you have to enter into my Heaven, what would you say?' "

Kennedy's response in that bedroom, alone by himself, was: "Well I've tried to live a good life and I've done the best I could. I've kept the Ten Commandments and I've followed the Golden Rule." Then Kennedy relates: "And Dr. Barnhouse said to me, or at least it seemed that way, 'Young man, if you had had the audacity to say such a thing as that to the All-Holy God who knows your every thought and deed, he would have instantly plunged you into the Lake of Fire!' "

Kennedy, lying in his bed, said he was shocked by the preacher's words. Kenney thought: "Well, my entire toothpick castle of theology collapsed to the floor and I realized that I didn't have any hope. For the first time in my life I was lost. I didn't know how to get home. Now, I had been lost for 23 years, I just never knew it before. He went on to tell the Gospel and he said the most astonishing thing. He said that eternal life was a free gift, that Jesus Christ had paid for it with his own suffering and blood on the Cross and God offered it graciously, freely to all of those who would trust in Christ."[4]

That's Good News!

Paul reminds Titus as to how we are *not* saved: "he saved us, not because of works done by us in righteousness . . ." (3:5).

Mercy

Next, Paul tells us what the motivating cause and attitude of God is in saving us: "he saved us . . . according to his own mercy . . ." (3:3).

Reflecting on his own conversion experience when writing to Pastor Timothy, Paul says, "I thank [God] who has given me strength, Christ Jesus our Lord, because he judged me faithful, appointing me to his service, though formerly I was a blasphemer, persecutor, and insolent opponent. But I received mercy . . ." (1 Tim. 1:12 -13).

Someone has said that grace is God giving us what we don't deserve, whereas mercy is God withholding from us what we do deserve—eternal death and hell. Oh, where would we be without a merciful God?! Calvary is mercy! The Cross is mercy! God's saving action in your life and mine is mercy.

Is it any wonder that William Newell (1868-1956) wrote these words some days following his conversion to Christ?

Oh, the love that drew salvation's plan!
Oh, the grace that brought it down to man!
Oh, the mighty gulf that God did span at Calvary!
Mercy there was great, and grace was free;

Pardon there was multiplied to me;
There my burdened soul found liberty – at Calvary.

We could fill volumes writing about the mercy of God — and God's thirsty-hearted followers have tried to do so since the beginning of time. Listen to these classic words penned by Frederick William Faber (1814-1863):

There's a wideness in God's mercy,
Like the wideness of the sea;
There's a kindness in His justice,
Which is more than liberty.

For the love of God is broader
Than the measure of our mind;
And the heart of the Eternal
Is most wonderfully kind.[6]

The Instruments in Our Salvation

Having spoken of God's motivating cause in our salvation — mercy — next Paul speaks of the instruments God uses in our salvation. "But when the goodness and loving kindness of God our Savior appeared, he saved us, not because of works done by us in righteousness, but according to his own mercy, by the washing of regeneration . . ." (3:5).

"Regeneration" is God's term for spiritual birth, new life, a birth from above, to be born anew, to be born again. God's saving act is brought about by infusing into the heart and life of repentant sinners new life, spiritual life, resurrection life, eternal life, the very life of the Lord Jesus Christ himself.

Sinners are walking dead men and women, spiritual corpses. They have biological life, but they are void of spiritual life. Many of these people are religious corpses, many are pagan corpses. Many of these corpses sit in a pew week after week, and many never walk through the doors of a church and have no intention of doing so. But of all of these it can be said in the words of Augustine, "Thou hast made us for thyself, O Lord, and our heart is restless until it finds its rest in thee."

A few years ago I was captivated by some words written by C. S. Lewis, words on this subject of dead people coming to life. He likens them to statues. He wrote, "This world is a great sculptor's shop. We are the statues and there is a rumor going round the shop that some of us are some day going to come to life."[7] I couldn't get that conversion metaphor out of my mind, so I wrote the following.

A room filled with statues:
  all uniquely beautiful,
    chiseled and hammered,
      made out of stone.

There were ears and eyes,
  hands and feet.
    But they had no sight;
      they did not feel or walk.

They were cold and lifeless stones;
  they could not respond.
    Void of love and devotion,
      they stared, merely stared.

Then without notice
  there came a gentle Wind blowing.
    The stones became warm;
      they could now hear and see.

Walking out of the room
  into the loving embrace
    of their Sculptor,
      they cried, "Father!"

I think of the conversion of Charles Colson, the ex-presidential aid, who came to Christ after he was implicated in the infamous Watergate debacle. Of his conversion event he wrote, "that Friday morning, while I sat alone staring at the sea I love, words that I had not been certain I could understand or say fell naturally from my lips: 'Lord Jesus, I believe you. I accept you. Please come into my life. I commit it to you.'" And then he wrote something that is so typical of the new life in Christ Jesus. He says, "With these few words that morning, while the briny sea churned, came a sureness of mind that matched the depth of feeling in my heart. There came something more: strength and serenity, a wonderful new assurance about life, fresh perception of myself and the world around me. In the process, I felt old fears, tensions, and animosities draining away. I was coming alive to things I had never seen before . . ."[8]

Conversion is a new life.

Furthermore, Paul uses the language of "washing" in conjunction with regeneration: "he saved us, not because of works done by us in righteousness, but according to his own mercy, by the **washing** of regeneration . . ." (3:5).

The washing of water baptism is a symbol of the washing of regeneration. Baptism and regeneration are not synonymous. One is a symbol; the other is the substance. The one is a sign; the other reality. God says when he saves us, imparting spiritual life to us, there is a simultaneous *washing* which occurs.

What is washed? Our very consciences, our hearts – that inner, deep spiritual entity from which thoughts, choices, imaginations rise. King David's confession and plea to God following his dreadful sins was, "wash me, and I shall be whiter than snow" (Ps. 51:7). Using the symbolism of the sacrificial blood sprinkled on the mercy seat and the water the high priest washed himself with before entering the Holy of Holies, the author of the *Letter to the Hebrews* speaks of those who have their "hearts sprinkled from an evil conscience and [their] bodies washed with pure water" (Heb. 10:22).

Washing – a clean conscience, a clean heart – now ready to live a clean life, by the power of the indwelling Christ.

Conversion is a washed life.

Now for the second instrument in God's saving grace, working in the lives of repentant sinners: "he saved us, not because of works done by us in righteousness, but according to his own mercy, by the washing of regeneration and renewal of the Holy Spirit, whom he poured out on us richly through Jesus Christ our Savior . . ." (3:5-6).

There are two "re" words in this text. The one—"regeneration"— has to do with the *impartation* of new life, the very life of Christ; the other— "renewal"—has to do with *making* new, making new by the Holy Spirit. The new Christian not only experiences new life; he becomes a new life—from within to without. In the words of the apostle to the Corinthian Church: "if anyone is in Christ, he is a new creation. The old has passed away; behold, the new has come" (2 Cor. 5:17).

This renewal commences at a point in time—the new birth—and immediately begins the work of transforming the believer into the likeness of the Lord Jesus Christ. Paul uses the term in Romans 12:2: "Do not be conformed to this world, but be transformed by the renewal of your mind . . ."

Spiritual renewal, spiritual renovation, is an ongoing process by the indwelling Holy Spirit in the life of every Christian, and the Spirit requires our cooperation in this transformation. How does the Holy Spirit do this? How does he renew the Christian's heart and conduct? Let's go back to Titus 2:11-12.

Training Grace

The Spirit says through the Apostle Paul, "For the grace of God has appeared, bringing salvation for all people, training us to renounce ungodliness and worldly passions, and to live self-controlled, upright, and godly lives in the present age . . ."

Paul takes a very common Greek word of his time, which is used in the context of education. He is saying that the grace of God not only saves the sinner, but that the grace of God trains, teaches, educates every Christian—training us, teaching us, educating us.

What does this grace of God *train* the Christian to do? Paul mentions five areas that the grace of God trains us in. First, he identifies two negatives.

Renounce ungodliness. Ungodliness is just the opposite of godliness. The Holy Spirit trains the Christian to reject, forsake, turn his back on, renounce—every attitude and known action and activity which does not measure up to Christlike attitudes and behavior. The indwelling Holy Spirit performs this work in our conscience as we read God's Word and hear it preached, and sometimes he performs this work in our conscience when, at the time, we may have no specific knowledge of his Word in a particular area, but he always impresses us to act in harmony with his Word.

Renounce worldly passions. The Holy Spirit trains us to renounce every love, affection, attachment, devotion, and passion which is incompatible with our new life in Christ. We are called to hate what God hates and to love what God loves. We are called to love the Lord our God with all of our heart, soul, mind, and strength. Any affection and attachment which interferes with his love in us must be renounced. Whatever is a passion for things must be exchanged for a passion for Christ.

Paul calls these "worldly passions." There are many *passions* or *desires* in which it is both entirely natural and acceptable for a Christian to exercise and fulfill. But these passions and desires are considered "worldly" whenever they are not brought under the lordship of Jesus Christ and exercised in keeping with the plain teaching of God's written Word.

For example, the desire to worship must be reserved for the only one and true God and Father of the Lord Jesus Christ. Otherwise it is idolatry, which is generated by an innate desire to worship but is worldly because it fails to focus on the one true God. The same can be said for sexual desires. These passions are considered worldly when engaged in outside the bonds of marriage between a male and female. God says the Christian is to renounce worldly passions.

Secondly, the apostle identifies three positive spheres of behavior the Holy Spirit — the grace of God — trains us in.

Self-control. "For the grace of God has appeared, bringing salvation for all people, training us . . . to live self-controlled . . . lives in the present age . . ."

The Spirit trains the Christian to control his and her temper, eyes, ears, tongues, stomachs — the natural urges. Paul says elsewhere, the fruit of the Spirit is "self-control" (Gal. 5:23).

Fallen man can only go so far in controlling his natural appetites, desires, and instincts. He needs outside help, help from above.

Uprightness. "For the grace of God has appeared, bringing salvation for all people, training us . . . to live upright . . . lives in the present age . . ."

Before God's regenerating, renewing grace entered our lives, many of us may have lived good lives as the world counts goodness, but we did not—because we could not—live lives pleasing to God, according to his standard of righteousness.

Paul says in chapter one of this letter, that the Cretans had a reputation for lying, practicing evil, laziness, and gluttony. He said even one of their own pagan philosophers accused them of such behavior. Christians are called out of the world's mindset to be different.

Will Thomas was just a new convert when his longtime friend Art (prior to his own conversion) thought he would test his friend's new-found "religion." Will was visiting Art in his home. Art went into his bedroom and came out with a pornographic magazine. He opened it and thrust it into the face of Will and said, "There, look at that!" Will's response? "Art, I don't look at that stuff anymore." Art said after his own conversion, "I knew Will had the real thing." God's grace was training Will in uprightness.

Godliness. "For the grace of God has appeared, bringing salvation for all people, training us . . . to live godly lives in the present age . . ."

Christians must be known by more of what they *do* than what they *don't* do; by what they *engage in* than what they *refrain* from; what not only they *oppose,* but what they're *for*; not for only by what they *reject,* but for what they *embrace.* One who knew him most intimately, said of the Lord Jesus, he was "full of grace and truth" (John 1:14). Godliness covers the entire spectrum of living for the Christian.

The Spirit trains us as to how to walk in humility before God and one another. How to walk in love with the people of God and our neighbors. How to strive to live in peace with all people. How to be forbearing and forgiving, patient and longsuffering, merciful and compassionate, thoughtful, kind, and considerate.

Some of the evidences of the Spirit's renewal and training are immediate in the new convert. But not always. We never graduate from this school. The Spirit's training is always active and present—throughout our earthly pilgrimage. The Lord Jesus said, "My sheep hear my voice, and I know them, and they follow me" (John. 10:27).

Are you saved from your sins? Are you one of the Good Shepherd's sheep? Are you listening to his voice? Are you following him? Have you been washed? Are you being renewed? Are you cooperating with God as he trains you?

Possibly these words, written by a Scottish minister by the name of Horatius Bonar (1808-1889) in the nineteenth century, will mean something to you as I close this two-part series. The opening words of his hymn reads:

I was a wandering sheep,
I did not love the fold;
I did not love my Shepherd's voice,
I would not be controlled.

But after the author takes us through his personal conversion to Christ, the ninth stanza of the hymn reads:

No more a wandering sheep,
I love to be controlled;
I love my tender Shepherd's voice,
I love the peaceful fold.[9]

I pray that each person who happens to read this chapter will, if not presently, soon experience the reality which lies behind those words.

Grace be with you.

CHAPTER 4

Total Consecration
(Part 1)

In twentieth-century Christianity we have replaced the expression
"total surrender" with the word "commitment," and "slave" with
"servant." But there is an important difference. A servant gives
service to someone, but a slave belongs to someone. We commit our-
selves to do something, but when we surrender ourselves to some-
one, we give ourselves.[1]

The Hebrew and Greek words for "consecrate," or one of its forms, occur approximately 199 times in the Bible: 171 in the Old Testament and 28 times in the New Testament.[2] The first occurrence where the word is rendered "consecrate" is found in Exodus 13:2, where God commanded Israel: "Consecrate [*quadash*] to me all the firstborn. Whatever is the first to open the womb among the people of Israel, both of man and of beast, is mine" (Ex. 13:2).[3]

The two occurrences in the New Testament where the ESV renders the Greek word (*hagiazō*) as "consecrate" are located in John's Gospel and are spoken by Jesus. In the first occurrence, Jesus is responding to the Jews' charge that Jesus had committed blasphemy by saying that he and the Father were one: "If he called them gods to whom the word of God came—and Scripture cannot be broken—do you say of him whom the Father consecrated [*hēgiasen*] and sent into the world, 'You are blaspheming,' because I said, 'I am the Son of God'?" (John 10:36). The second occurrence is located in Jesus' prayer for his disciples: "And for their sake I consecrate [*hagiazō*] myself, that they also may be sanctified in truth" (John 17:19).

The term "consecrate," as used in the Old and New Testaments, has at least four shades of meaning according to *A Greek-English Lexicon of the New Testament and Other Early Christian Literature*.[4]

• It means to "set aside something or make it suitable for ritual purposes;" i.e. "to consecrate, dedicate" things. For example, when God gave instructions to Moses regarding the consecration of Aaron and the priests, he said, "You shall consecrate them, that they may be most holy. Whatever touches them will become holy" (Ex. 30:29).

• It means to "include a person in the inner circle of what is holy in both cultic and moral associations of the word, *consecrate, dedicate, sanctify*." For example, when Moses was instructed by God to provide special garments for the priests to minister in, God told him: "And you shall put them on Aaron your brother, and on his sons with him, and shall anoint them and ordain them and consecrate them, that they may serve me as priests" (Ex. 28:41). In Hebrews the writer uses the same Greek word in reference to ritual purity: "For if the sprinkling of defiled persons with the blood of goats and bulls and with the ashes of a heifer sanctifies [*hagiazei*] for the purification of the flesh, . . ." (Heb. 9:13).

• The word is used to mean to treat persons and things as holy. For example, Peter exhorts Christians to "regard Christ the Lord as holy [*hagiasate*], always being prepared to make a defense to anyone who asks you for a reason for the hope that is in you" (1 Pet. 3:15).

• Finally, it means to "eliminate that which is incompatible with holiness, *purify*." For example, Paul expresses his desire for the Thessalonian believers by praying, "Now may the God of peace himself sanctify [*hagiasai*] you completely, and may your whole spirit and soul and body be kept blameless at the coming of our Lord Jesus Christ" (1 Thess. 5:23).

For the purposes of this section of the chapter, the term consecration is used to describe the follower of the Lord Jesus Christ; one who has surrendered himself completely to his Master and Lord, without reservation, for the purpose of living a life wholly devoted to the Lord Jesus to the glory of God. It is the call to follow Jesus with wholehearted devotion. It includes the totality of the person — body, soul, and spirit.

Such an offering in total consecration to the Lord Jesus has been beautifully expressed in the classic prayer of Frances Havergal. The first verse reads:

> *Take my life, and let it be*
> *Consecrated, Lord, to thee;*
> *Take my moments and my days,*
> *Let them flow in ceaseless praise.*[5]

The Example of Abraham

The giving of oneself to Christ in total consecration is explicitly taught in the NT as well as with many pointers in the OT. There is an outstanding example from the life of Abraham that speaks to this subject of total consecration. When God first called Abraham, he called him to leave his homeland and relatives and travel to unknown territory. Abraham (then called Abram) responded to God's initiative by obeying: "So Abram went, as the LORD had told him" (Gen. 12:4). Abraham continued to walk with God, albeit, with some occasional questionable behavior.[6] Nevertheless, aside from a few recorded lapses in moral judgment, Abraham's life was characterized by the faithful worship of and obedience to Yahweh.

Abraham's pilgrimage with Yahweh reached a critical turning point, however, with respect to his love for Isaac, his son. Two loves and loyalties were in danger of competing, with one canceling out the other. Yahweh, Abraham's covenant God, devised a plan whereby the patriarch would offer that which was most precious to him as a gift to his LORD. God asked for the gift of Abraham's son, which in substance, was the giving of Abraham himself in total consecration to his God. "Take your son, your only son Isaac, whom you love, and go to the land of Moriah, and offer him there as a burnt offering on one of the mountains of which I will tell you" (Gen. 22:2). The record informs us that Abraham's obedient faith to Yahweh's call was immediate: "So Abraham rose early in the morning, saddled his donkey, and took two of his young men with him, and his son Isaac. And he cut the wood for the burnt offering and arose and went to the place of which God had told him" (Gen. 22:3).

Following a three-day journey, Abraham and Isaac reached their appointed destination. Leaving his servants at the mountain's base, father and son climbed Moriah's slope until the father is informed by Yahweh of the precise place where the offering is to occur. After making the necessary altar preparations, "Abraham bound Isaac his son and laid him on the altar, on top of the wood. Then Abraham reached out his hand and took the knife to slaughter his son." God saw that his consecration was complete and called out to his devoted follower: "'Abraham, Abraham!' And he said, 'Here am I.' He said, 'Do not lay your hand on the boy or do anything to him, for now I know that you fear God, seeing you have not withheld your son, your only son, from me'" (Gen. 22:11-12).

Consecration Involves Death

One of the masters in Spiritual theology in the nineteenth century was the devout Lutheran minister, George Steinberger. In a little volume that is considered a classic by many who have read it, this perceptive student of God's ways with men, said this about man's essential problem:

The fall of our first parents was a result of their making themselves the center of life. The soul who does this today will learn that spiritual darkness and death, separation from and enmity toward God, are the consequences. In all that is selfish, the power of Satan is active. In the selfish heart there burns the hidden fire of hell. As long as we cherish our own lives, we keep ourselves under God's curse; for on the cross God has cursed all that is selfish. To live for one's self is to be against God.

Steinberger then adds: "Flesh [in the moral sense, as used by Paul] is ingrown selfness" Intrinsic to total consecration to God is death—a deep death to one's sinful self-interest and every inordinate human attachment.

In offering his son Isaac to God, Abraham experienced a deep, inner personal *death* to his own preferences, affections, and desires. Jesus said such is the case for anyone who would be one of his authentic disciples. Our Lord radically taught that one cannot be his disciple while making his own self-centered choices. Matthew 16 records this truth following Christ's dramatic encounter with Peter. Jesus had just informed his disciples that his own future involved suffering, death, and resurrection. Peter only heard "suffering and death." Instinctively the disciple recoils from such a thought of hardship and death for Jesus (and for himself as well?). His instincts were to spare Christ of such a future. Taking Jesus aside, he tried to dissuade his Master from pursuing such a course. Jesus rebuked Peter: "Get behind me, Satan! You are a hindrance to me. For you are not setting your mind on the things of God, but on the things of man" (Matt. 16:23).

Christ turns the occasion into a teaching opportunity. He informs all his disciples that discipleship must embrace suffering and death: "If anyone would come after me, let him deny himself and take up his cross and follow me. For whoever would save his life will lose it, but whoever loses his life for my sake will find it" (Matt. 16:24-25).

To follow Jesus is to turn away from one's self and selfish ways. "Jesus is giving us a way," observes Frederick Bruner, "to loose ourselves from 'being gripped by the concerns of human beings' (Matt. 16:23), and that way is decisively to disown ourselves and the lordship of our own thinking and to go under new management. Self-denial is not so much giving up chocolates at Lent as it is giving up on ourselves as lords; it is the decision to let another Lord rule one's life."[8]

Christ's disciples must reject their inborn bent to self-sovereignty and self-rule. In the words of Dietrich Bonhoeffer (1906-1945), "When Christ calls a man, he bids him come and die."[9] Such a death embraces every choice the disciple of Jesus makes. Exhorting the disciples of Christ of his own day, Bonhoeffer said: "You must not follow the work which you choose, not the suffering which you devise, but that which comes to you against your choice, thoughts, and desires."[10]

Such a radical death to sin and self was objectively wrought for every Christian in Christ's substitutionary, atoning death, but must be appropriated by faith in order to be effectively realized in the heart and life of Christ's disciples in every age. Paul teaches this truth in the great Romans 6 passage. In verse 6 he announces, "We know that our old self was crucified with him in order that the body of sin might be brought to nothing, so that we would no longer be enslaved to sin." Paul is saying since Christ has achieved such a great victory for the believer through his death and resurrection, the believer must not be content to continue in sin, but must now live in obedience to Christ. How can this be done? Paul provides the answer in Romans 6:11-12:

So you also must consider yourselves dead to sin and alive to God in Christ Jesus. Let not sin therefore reign in your mortal bodies, to make you obey their passions. Do not present your members to sin as instruments for unrighteousness, but present yourselves to God as those who have been brought from death to life, and your members to God as instruments for righteousness.[24]

Here death is directly linked to consecration—a death to sin and the offering of oneself to God.

While Jesus was sinless—having no inherent proclivities to self-centeredness—nonetheless, he is the disciple's perfect model in how death to one's human preferences opens the door to blessing, usefulness, and fruitfulness in the kingdom of God.

One day there were some Greeks who approached the disciple Philip, inquiring how they might gain an audience with Jesus. Philip and Andrew carried the Greeks' request to their Lord. After listening to Philip reiterate their request, Jesus spoke of his impending death in picturesque language: "The hour has come for the Son of Man to be glorified. Truly, truly, I say to you, unless a grain of wheat falls into the earth and dies, it remains alone; but if it dies, it bears much fruit. Whoever loves his life loses it, and whoever hates his life in this world will keep it for eternal life" (John 12:23-25). By saying no to his own preferences as well as his very life, Jesus presented his body in consecration to his heavenly Father, thus making it possible for all peoples of all time to enjoy eternal life. The writer of Hebrews captures this beautifully in chapter 10:5-7):

Consequently, when Christ came into the world, he said,

"Sacrifices and offerings you have not desired, but a body have you prepared for me; in burnt offerings and sin offerings you have taken no pleasure." Then I said, "Behold, I have come to do your will, O God, as it is written of me in the scroll of the book."

As painful as it may be to man's fallen ego, an existential inner death must occur before the disciple can adequately give himself in total consecration to Christ. Until such a death takes place, one lives with a divided heart and mind; he is torn between his love for Christ and his love for lesser things. Quoting Augustine, François Fénelon writes, "When we love anything out of [i.e., separate from] God, . . . we love God the less for it." Then Fénelon remarks, "It is like a stream from which part of the water is turned off. This division of the affections of the heart diminishes what should go to God, and it is from such a division that arise all the disturbances of the heart. God wishes to have all, and his jealousy will not leave a divided heart in peace.[11]

David prayed that God would cure his own divided heart: "unite my heart to fear your name" (Psa. 86:11). The apostle James called Christians to such a radical self-renunciation, a calling that demanded a break from everything that threatened one's supreme loyalty to Jesus Christ: "purify your hearts you double-minded" (James 4:8).

Pentecost Preparation

To the careful student of God's Word, Pentecost was clearly a transforming event to all who were present in that Upper Room. A radical cleansing and empowering accompanied the Spirit's descent. While the veil has not been lifted for us to peer into much that occurred during those ten days prior to the Spirit's outpouring, one thing that surely did occur was a renewed consecration by the disciples to their Lord. What happened at Pentecost attests to this, for God does not cleanse and fill with his Spirit anyone who is not totally surrendered and consecrated to him.

What about you, my friend? Have you given yourself totally to Christ. Have you experienced what Oswald Chambers (1874-1917) termed a "white funeral"? Or do some pockets of resistance remain? If Christ is not truly your Lord, seek a quiet place and stay there until both your consecration and the renovation of your heart is complete.

As lovely as it may be to the eyes,
 a lone grain is worthless unless it dies;
But if it falls hidden into the ground,
 from death eventually it will abound.

To save myself is but to lose my life —
 self-sovereignty is a kingdom of grief.
But to lose myself is to gain with God,
 and to take the path that Jesus trod.

Our Lord led the way by the death he died;
 surrendered fully, he was crucified.
What seemed that Day to be a tragic loss,
 was in fact total triumph through the Cross.

If I am to live life to the fullest,
 wanting to see an abundant harvest,
Like him I must fall like a grain of wheat —
 into the ground before the Mercy Seat.

Renouncing my prideful, self-centered way,
 in full surrender I sign my life away.
Entrusting to Him my past and future;
 rising from the ground in the Spirit's pow'r.

CHAPTER 5

Total Consecration
(Part 2)

When the convicted sinner responds to the Spirit's call to repent of his sins and believe on the Lord Jesus Christ for his own salvation, he is by virtue of his own sins and sinfulness, overwhelmed and fundamentally preoccupied with his personal guilt and condemnation. Thus, while his volitional and emotional response to the gospel call may vary, depending on the measure of his spiritual knowledge, his cry is universally expressed in the words of the convicted Philippian jailer: "Sirs, what must I do to be saved?" (Acts 16:31).[1]

The convicted sinner is concerned with how he might become rightly related to God. While he may not be acquainted with doctrinal terms such as justification and reconciliation, this is his need — to be justified by God and to be reconciled to God. His cry is for mercy, for forgiveness. The merciful God grants such a request to all who sincerely repent and trust in his Son, the Lord Jesus Christ. To such a contrite sinner, the words of the apostle ring true: "Therefore, since we have been justified by faith, we have peace with God through our Lord Jesus Christ" (Rom. 5:1).

For the justified believer, there remains no longer a record of indictment and condemnation of his sins before God: "There is therefore now no condemnation for those who are in Christ Jesus" (Rom. 8:1). A legal pardon has been issued on the basis of Christ's atoning death, forgiveness has been granted, a new status — "in Christ" — has been conferred, and the believer has been set apart ("sanctified") in Christ Jesus. These are judicial as well as experiential realties for the new Christian, plus so much more.

While, as we have previously stated in the last chapter, there is a measure of consecration involved for the believer when he first comes to Christ, it appears that for many believers there is an event of consecration that often follows one's personal conversion to Christ. While I am not interested in quibbling over what to call such an event (theories abound on this subject), to be true to the Scriptures as well as to the testimonies of many reputable Christians, one cannot dismiss such a deep post-conversion experience in a cavalier manner, as some are wont to do.

While this teaching of the total consecration of the believer is both implicit and explicit throughout the New Testament in particular, I want to examine Romans 12:1 in exploring this subject more fully.

In the first eight chapters of Romans, Paul has addressed the following subjects: all people are under the universal wrath and condemnation of God—Jew and Gentiles alike; no one can achieve a right standing with God on the basis of his own righteousness; God took the initiative in bringing sinful man into a right relationship with himself by offering his Son, the Lord Jesus Christ, as an atoning sacrifice for sin. Those who repent of their sins and believe on Jesus Christ are declared to be right with God, that is, justified. As justified persons, they have been released from the Law's bondage so that they may live in the power of the Spirit. Following his explication of the role of Israel in God's economy in chapters 9-11, Paul urges his readers in 12:1, to offer themselves in full consecration to God.

Romans 12:1

Paul's exhortation: "I appeal to you therefore, brothers, by the mercies of God, to present your bodies as a living sacrifice, holy and acceptable to God, which is your spiritual worship."

Who are these readers with respect to the gospel? To whom is the apostle making such an appeal? There are several reasons for believing these readers are authentic disciples of the Lord Jesus Christ:

- Paul's greeting to the recipients of this Roman letter makes it clear that his appeal in Romans 12:1 is directed to those who have already come to faith in the Lord Jesus Christ: those "who are called to belong to Jesus Christ" and to "all those in Rome who are loved by God and called to be saints" (Rom. 1:6-7).

• Throughout this letter, there are ten specific instances where Paul addresses his readers with the fraternal designation of "brothers."[2] The term "brothers," as noted by Joseph Fitzmyer, "has nothing to do with . . . blood relationship or kinship; it designates the closeness experienced by those who were followers of the risen Christ and a sense of the intimate relations that Paul has with those he so addresses."[3] This Christian communal relationship transcends all gender, ethnic, and racial groupings.

• Chapters 6-8 are clearly an appeal to those who are justified and are not in the "flesh" but in the "Spirit."

• The ethical exhortations Paul gives in chapters 12-16 clearly have Christians in view. It is unthinkable that non-Christians could possibly respond to such imperatives.

God desires our *all*. If one is to live a life of cultivating and expressing a passionate love for the Lord Jesus Christ, he can only do so if he has given himself entirely to Christ. Such a dedication to God is intensely personal and real. In view of this, let no one suppose that he receives a *partial* Christ in the conversion experience, and a *complete* Christ in a post-conversion experience. It is not a matter of accepting Jesus as "Savior" in the conversion experience, and making him "Lord" in a post-conversion experience, but is a matter of one's spiritual condition and need before and after the conversion event.

The eighteenth century spiritual master Jean-Pierre de Caussade, a French Jesuit priest understood this like few others. He came to understand the importance of making a total surrender of oneself to God if the Christian is to live a life of love to the glory of God. Inviting his fellow believers to make such a surrender, he wrote,

Come not to study the theory of God's grace, or to learn what it has done in the past and is still doing, but simply to be open yourself to what it can do. You do not need to know what it has said to others, or repeat words intended only for them which you have overheard. His grace will speak to you, yourself, what is best for you.[4]

While we may not want to go as far as Caussade went in seemingly discounting God's work in others, both past and present, what Caussade is emphasizing is the need for the believer to deal personally with God. The specifics of such a consecration are uniquely personal to the individual believer.

Paul urges these believers in Romans 12:1 "by the mercies of God, to present your bodies as a living sacrifice, holy and acceptable to God, which is your spiritual worship." Having reviewed God's sovereign purposes for Israel in God's economy in chapters 9-11, and noting the failure of these people to accept God's covenant purposes for them through the Lord Jesus Christ, Paul makes a strong appeal to his readers not to follow in the footsteps of these unbelievers, nor to be presumptuous.

This is the purpose of the "therefore." In other words, on the basis of what he has previously addressed, "therefore," these believers must learn from their Jewish brothers and not make a similar mistake. It is the mercy of God that the Gentiles have been made partakers of the gospel. These readers should not presume upon God's mercies; after all, Paul says, "Just as you were at one time disobedient to God but now have received mercy because of their disobedience, so they too have now been disobedient in order that by the mercy shown to you they also may now receive mercy. For God has consigned all to disobedience, that he may have mercy on all" (Rom. 11:30-32). Because of the unfathomable mercies that God has shown these believers in Jesus Christ, the apostle urges them to make a full consecration. Paul "knows — not least from his own experience — ," says John Stott, "that there is no greater incentive to holy living than a contemplation of the mercies of God."[5]

The form of the word "present" in Romans 12:1 (*parastēsai*) is an aorist infinitive, and is significant. Of this tense, New Testament scholar C. F. D. Moule (1908-2007) said, "the chief function of the aorist tense is to indicate an action viewed as instantaneous . . . , no matter whether present, future, or past."[6] In other words, Paul is appealing to his readers to make a definitive total consecration of themselves to God. He is urging them to do something that only they can do by an act of the will, assisted of course, by the strength of the Spirit. This is the human side of the work of sanctification. God can only sanctify what man consecrates. This held true under the Old Covenant regarding material things—for example, the Temple furnishings; and it is true under the New Covenant as well. On one occasion, Jesus spoke of the altar sanctifying those gifts presented in the Temple (see Matt. 23:19).

Fritz Rienecker suggests the word "present" in Romans 12:1 is a "technical term for presenting a sacrifice, literally meaning 'to place beside.'"[7] Joseph Fitzmyer makes the same observation. He says the verb "not only means to place something at the disposition of another but also has the nuance of 'offering, presenting' something as a sacrifice." Then he notes, "Whereas the Jewish sacrifice implied the slaughter of what was offered, Paul uses the verb figuratively of Christian life and activity."[8]

What Paul says is to be consecrated—presented—by these Christians to God is their "bodies." The New Testament (Paul in particular) has much to say about the corporeality of man. While much of Gnosticism considered the body inherently evil and incapable of redemption, the Christian ethic held that the body was to be regarded as the temple of the Holy Spirit, and that Christians were to glorify God by what their bodies were actively engaged in. Thus, Paul argued against the Christian engaging in any kind of sexual immorality because the body "is meant for the Lord, and the Lord for the body" (see 1 Cor. 6:12-20). Furthermore, Paul says there will come a day when all believers will appear before the judgment seat of Christ to give an account of "what [they have] done in the body, whether good or evil" (2 Cor. 5:10). Moreover, the Christian's response to the promise of God's desire to dwell among his people, and his consequent command that they should not defile themselves with any "unclean thing,"—is to "cleanse ourselves from every defilement of the body and spirit, bringing holiness to completion in the fear of God" (2 Cor. 7:1). Paul said it was his desire that Christ would always be "honored in my body" (Phil. 1:20).

To show how highly God values the body, Paul says that at the Parousia, "the Lord Jesus Christ . . . will transform our lowly body to be like his glorious body" (Phil. 3:20-21). It is because of this view of the body in first-century Christianity that Thomas Oden can state, the "body is greatly honored in Christianity, not only in the incarnation, which is the coming of God in the flesh, but the resurrection as well, which is the reuniting of the human body-soul."[9]

It is from this divine perspective of the importance of man's body that the apostle exhorts these Christians to make a complete consecration of their "bodies" to God. In saying "bodies," Paul is not placing the body in opposition to the soul/heart of man—his will, affections, and so forth. He is simply stating that when the body is consecrated to God, it represents man's total consecration to God. Matthew Henry (1662-1714) believed when Paul uses "bodies" here, he means "your whole selves."[10] On the other hand, Bishop Handley Moule (1841-1920) believed when Paul used "bodies" he meant specifically "bodies," not "your spirit, intelligence, feelings or aspirations, but *'your bodies'* to your Lord."[11]

Let it be said, that while the consecration of man to God includes the total person, it would seem that Paul specifically has in mind the consecration of man's body *per se*, which of course, does not exclude man's soul and spirit.[12]

The "bodies" are to be presented/consecrated to God as living sacrifices in contrast to the former Covenant's *dead* sacrifices. The "bodies," furthermore, are to be presented to God as "holy, and acceptable to God, which is your spiritual worship."

The use of the word "holy" (*hagian*) in one's presentation/ consecration of the body to God is a further argument that Paul is addressing authentic Christian believers and not unbelievers. A non-Christian cannot make a presentation of a "holy" body to God. We must ask then, *How is it that a Christian can make an offering of a "holy" body to God?* In this way: because the Christian has already been "set apart" (sanctified in Christ Jesus) to live a holy life."[13]

Since the believer has been definitively sanctified (set apart to live a holy life) in Christ when he was justified and regenerated, he subsequently is to make that sanctification *actual* by a giving himself in total consecration to the Lord Jesus Christ. On this matter, John Murray (1898-1975) commented,

> Holiness is contrasted here with the defilement which characterizes the body of sin and with all sensual lust. Holiness is the fundamental character and to be well-pleasing ["acceptable"] to God the governing principle of a believer. These qualities have reference to his body as well as to his spirit and show how ethical character belongs to the body and to its functions. No terms could certify this fact more than "holy" and "well-pleasing to God."[14]

This appeal by the apostle to the Roman disciples of Christ of his day left every believer with a sobering choice: to be Christ's total person, or to shrink into a lesser kind of spiritual existence and apathy. For the one who truly desires to cultivate and express a passionate love for Christ, the answer to such a choice is apparent. This is the reason why a total consecration to Christ is such a critical foundational element in the cultivation and expression of a passionate love for our Lord. The making of such a consecration has been beautifully expressed in the words of Mary James (1810-1883):

All for Jesus, all for Jesus!
All my being's ransomed powers:
All my thoughts and words and doings,
All my days and all my hours.

Let my hands perform His bidding,
Let my feet run in His ways;
Let my eyes see Jesus only,
Let my lips speak forth His praise.[15]

Be assured, what we wholeheartedly offer to God, God graciously accepts. If you haven't already done so, will you offer yourself today — totally to God? If you have previously done so, will you join with me just now in affirming the consecration of your total self to our holy and loving heavenly Father? □

CHAPTER 6

The Pure in Heart
(Part 1)

Self-made religion fears the message of Jesus—"Blessed are the pure in heart" (Matt. 5:8)[1]—because self-made religion is *manufactured*, thus it is forced from an impure heart, a heart that is an enemy of truth and of God's holy love.

Self-made religion obtains its security in rules and regulations for *supposed* holy living; its motto is "Do not handle. Do not taste. Do not touch" (Col. 2:21). This motto—paraded as a sanctimonious placard—creeps into testimonies, church manuals and sermons. It is incapable of wearing a disguise, for *self* is at the center.

Self-made religion is nothing but sinful pride held captive to appearances; it is in reality a monstrous projection of an unsanctified ego and an idolized self. It is a religion without the Cross; it is a religion without the Holy Spirit. Perceiving itself to be beautiful, it is ugly; perceiving itself to be holy, it is wicked.

True Christianity on the other hand is a religion of the heart, a heart that has been sprinkled clean by the atoning sacrificial blood of the Lamb of God; a heart purified by the Pentecostal Flame of the Holy Spirit. Any religion and message that falls short of preaching this two-fold truth—cleansing the conscience from the guilt of sin, and purifying the heart of entrenched self-centeredness,[2] is a defective and deficient propagation of the complete gospel of the Lord Jesus Christ.

Calvary and Pentecost meet fallen and twisted mankind at his deepest need. Through the Cross of Christ and the interpenetrating Holy Spirit, man is reconciled to God, forgiven of his sins, receives the very life of Christ, is indwelt by a Power coming down from above, and is made pure — both in God's sight as well as existentially. The Lord said it would be so when he spoke through the Old Testament prophets.

Old Testament Pointers

Using Isaiah as his mouthpiece in the seventh century B.C., the Lord foretold of a day of unprecedented and unparalleled heart purity (Isa. 36:25-27):

"I will sprinkle clean water on you, and you shall be clean from all your uncleannesses, and from all your idols I will cleanse you. And I will give you a new heart, and a new spirit I will put within you. And I will remove the heart of stone from your flesh and give you a heart of flesh. And I will put my Spirit within you, and cause you to walk in my statutes and be careful to obey my rules.

Writing some five hundred years before the Incarnation, the Lord revealed to Daniel about a time when "Many will be purified, made spotless and refined, . . ." (12:10 NIV). Approximately one hundred years later, the prophet Malachi is informed that in the coming dispensation, the Lord will perform his ministry "like a refiner's fire and like fullers' soap. He will sit as a refiner and purifier of silver, and he will purify the sons of Levi and refine them like gold and silver, and they will bring offerings in righteousness to the LORD" (3:2-3). The prophet who bridged both Covenants, John the Baptist, said of the consummate Baptizer, the Lord Jesus Christ, "He will baptize you with the Holy Spirit and fire. His winnowing fork is in his hand, and he will clear his threshing floor and gather his wheat into his barn, but the chaff he will burn with unquenchable fire" (Matt. 3:11-12).

Note again the purity God promises to accomplish through the coming Christ and the Holy Spirit:

"I will sprinkle clean water on you, and you shall be clean

from all your uncleannesses, and from all your idols I will cleanse you. And I will give you a new heart, . . ."

"Many will be purified, made spotless and refined, . . ."

"He will sit as a refiner and purifier of silver, and he will purify the sons of Levi and refine them like gold and silver, . . ."

"He will baptize you with the Holy Spirit and fire. His winnowing fork is in his hand, and he will clear his threshing floor and gather his wheat into his barn, but the chaff he will burn with unquenchable fire."

The prophets employed the symbols of water, fire, laundry soap, and a winnowing fork to illustrate the Messianic ministry of the Son of Man and the dynamic ministry of the Holy Spirit. Water, fire, and soap are all cleansing, purifying agents. The winnowing fork was a separating agent—cleansing the chaff from the wheat—a "sanctifying" agent, if you will.

When the Master announced to his followers on the Galilean slope that day, "Blessed are the pure in heart," he was not holding before them an idyllic, impossible status to be *achieved* through human effort, but the ushering in of a new dynamic to be *received*. It was through his rent body and poured out Spirit that defeated, broken humanity was to be made whole. Hearts made hard by sin and sinning, wills debilitated by broken promises and good intentions, divided souls incapable of pleasing the Master—would be healed and cured by Christ's broken body and shed blood, by the Holy Spirit's indwelling and heart cleansing. "I will give you a new heart;" "Many will be purified"; "He will sit as a refiner and purifier;" "the chaff he will burn with unquenchable fire."

Clear at the Center

The "heart" in Hebrew psychology is literally the center of human personality, the home of personal thinking, desiring, imagination, intention, and willing (heart, will, and mind are essentially one and the same in biblical thought). Theologian Frederick Bruner says we can "translate 'pure in heart,' . . . as 'clear at the center.'"[3]

This reminds me of the metaphor of "light" that both Jesus and the apostle John used in connection with purity of heart and holiness of life. For example, Jesus once said, "The eye is the lamp of your body; when your eye is clear, your whole body also is full of light; but when it is bad, your body is full of darkness. . . . If therefore your whole body is full of light, with no part dark part in it, it will be totally illumined, as when the lamp illumines you with its rays" (Luke 11:34, 36 NASB).

This is a powerful truth the Lord Jesus not only shared with his listeners two thousand years ago, but a real and necessary truth he reiterates to all who will listen today. He says some have a "clear" eye and some have a "bad" or an "evil" eye. Those possessing a "clear" eye are "full of light"; those possessing a "bad" eye are "full of darkness." And those who are "full of light" are "totally illumined" ["wholly bright" ESV].

Can we not logically deduce from the above that a "clear" eye is only made possible because the *heart* has first been made "clear," and the reason many eyes are "bad" is because the heart is "bad"? To repeat Bruner, to be pure in heart is to be "clear at the center" of one's person. And when one is clear at the center then the whole body is totally illumined, wholly bright.

Our Lord's use here of the "body" in Luke 11:34, 36, of course, encompasses the totality of one's conduct. The body is the instrument of the heart; it acts as the heart dictates. If the heart is bad, evil actions result. Thus the rationale for Christ's words in Mark 7:20-22: "What comes out of a person is what defiles him. For from within, out of the heart of man, come evil thoughts, sexual immorality, theft, murder, adultery, coveting, wickedness, deceit, sensuality, envy, slander, pride, foolishness."

More than Absence — Presence

To have a pure heart is to be cleansed of that which is foreign to our humanity. In the words of the prophets it is to be cleansed from our uncleannesses, and from all our idols; it is to be cleansed of a stony heart.

But heart purity is more than the absence of "foreign matter," it is the presence of the Holy One — the Holy Spirit. When the Holy Spirit arrives, he brings with him a new heart, a new spirit, a heart of flesh (i.e., a soft heart as opposed to a heart of stone), and a new power — "I will put my Spirit within you, and cause you to walk in my statutes and be careful to obey my rules" (Ezk. 36:27). It is not enough to be cleansed of unrighteousness, iniquity and sin. God desires to fill us with the new "corn and wine" of his rule and reign: "For the kingdom of God is . . . righteousness and peace and joy in the Holy Spirit" (Rom. 14:17).

The pure in heart "see" God, enjoy God, experience God. They are enabled to "see" God because they have "clear" eyes; they have clear eyes because they have a clear heart. Christ reigns without rival in such hearts.

Dynamic, Not Static

Does all of this mean that the pure in heart experience no conflict, are without need of deeper and ongoing cleansings? Not if I understand the Scriptures correctly or know anything about the human condition.

As long as he lives in this world, the pure-in-heart Christian will be in need of constant vigilance. The Master so warned: "Therefore be careful lest the light in you be darkness" (Luke 11:35). Again, "Watch and pray that you may not enter into temptation. The spirit indeed is willing, but the flesh is weak" (Mk 14:38). Or, in the words of Paul: "But I say, walk by the Spirit, and you will not gratify the desires of the flesh" (Gal. 5:17). Jesus warned that light can become darkness, that it's possible to give in to temptation; and Paul said if we don't keep in step with the Spirit we will inevitably act according to the flesh. George Heath (1745-1822) understood this conflict when he prayed:

> *My soul, be on thy guard;*
> *Ten thousand foes arise;*
> *The hosts of sin are pressing hard*
> *To draw thee from the skies.*
>
> *O watch, and fight, and pray;*
> *The battle ne'er give o'er;*

Renew it boldly every day,
And help divine implore.

Never think the victory won,
Nor lay thine armor down;
The work of faith will not be done,
Till thou obtain the crown.

Fight on, my soul, till death
Shall bring thee to thy God;
He'll take thee, at thy parting breath
To His divine abode.

How can it be that the pure in heart are in need of periodic deeper cleansings? If the heart is pure, why does it need additional cleansings? After all, isn't there such a thing as a cleansed-once-for-all experience? I know of none and I don't believe the Bible teaches such. The shores of disillusionment and disappointment are strewn with those who have sought and testified to such an experience, when afterward they discovered something alien in their "pure heart."

While "pure" means "pure," heart-purity must be maintained by the disciple's ongoing dynamic, personal relationship with the person of Jesus Christ, and not some illusory static experience to be kept in a "box." The Christian life is a walk, and in the course of this pilgrimage it remains the prerogative of our High Priest to reveal to us all things that are contrary to his holy love. A pure heart will humbly receive the Spirit's faithful corrections and attendant cleansings.

To illustrate: The late F. B. Meyer (1847-1929) was an able exponent of the Word of God. He excelled in the pulpit and had earned a reputation for being a godly, Spirit-filled Christian and preacher. He exhorted multitudes of believers to holy living, and earnestly endeavored to lead a careful life himself. However, at the height of his ministry he had a jolting experience.

While preaching to immense crowds in a convention, there arrived on the grounds a younger preacher and Bible teacher who was gaining considerable attention. Most of the crowds left Meyer's meetings, and began attending the services of Dr. G. Campbell Morgan

(1863-1949). For the first time in Meyer's ministerial career, he felt professional jealousy. He confessed such to a group of friends and said, "The only way I can conquer my feeling is to pray for him daily, which I do."[4]

The mightily used-of-God Scottish revivalist, Duncan Campbell (1898-1972), said on this subject, "Nowhere does the Word of God promise a once-for-all cleansing. We are to walk in the light if we are to know continuous cleansing. Let this be clearly understood and then we shall not fall into the error of trying to live today on the cleansing of yesterday."[5]

The Bible does not condone a "sinning religion." What the Bible does teach is this: God desires to give each of his people a pure heart, and it is only by walking in the light of God that he keeps pure what he first cleansed (1 John 1:7). The heart-cry of all of Christ's followers should be framed in the prayer of the famed Scottish pastor, Robert Murray M'Cheyne (1813-1843): "Lord, make me as holy as a pardoned sinner can be made."[6]

Be assured, my friend, God never creates a soul-thirst that he cannot satisfy.

Lord, it is not enough for me to have
  been cleansed once from sin and its pollution.
I need You each moment to keep me pure,
  as I humbly confess my condition.

CHAPTER 7

The Pure in Heart
(Part 2)

When pastoring in Upstate New York in the 1980s, the church scheduled Scottish evangelist Dr. John S. Logan for revival services on two occasions. In one of those services, this former chaplain to the Queen of England and successor to Oswald Chambers' pastorate in Leeds, England, related a tour he made with a group to a British coal mine one day. The thing that caught Logan's attention, he said, was the miners' eyes. After spending ten to twelve hours mining coal, with black dust particles saturating the underground cavern where they labored, upon their return to the top-side, although their clothing and bodies were totally covered with coal dust, their eyes were white, their eyes were clean.

Amazing, isn't it? The two members of the human body which are essential for working in a filthy, coal-black environment, our Creator-God designed a way in which tear ducts would continually provide the eyes with a lubricant to keep them clean. I ask you, if our wonderful Creator designed such mechanisms for the human eyes in order to keep them clean in such a black underworld, has he provided less for the heart of man through the atoning sacrifice of his Son and the blessed Holy Spirit?

The Scriptures inform us of the availability of a powerful cleansing through the vicarious death of the Lord Jesus Christ and the fiery baptism with the Holy Spirit. What God promises — heart purity — he wonderfully provides.

The Promise of Purity

In Part 1 of this series, we cited a few Old Testament promises that pointed to a coming day in which God said he would make provision for such heart purity that many of his people would later appropriate.

To reiterate:

"I will sprinkle clean water on you and you shall be clean from all your uncleanness, and from all your idols I will cleanse you" (Ezk. 36:25).[1]

"Many will be purified, made spotless and refined" (Dan. 12:10 NIV).

"For he is like a refiner's fire and like a fuller's soap. He will sit as a refiner and purifier of silver, and he will purify the sons of Levi and refine them like gold and silver, and they will bring offerings of righteousness to the LORD" (Mal. 3:2-3).

"I baptize you with water for repentance, but he who is coming after me is mightier than I, whose sandals I am not worthy to carry. He will baptize you with the Holy Spirit and fire" (Matt. 3:11).

This promised future purity for God's people is symbolically linked to three purifying agents: water, soap, and fire. God is saying that what these cleansers can accomplish in the physical world, I will accomplish through the Cross and Pentecost, through my beloved Son and indwelling Spirit in my thirsty-hearted disciples.

New Testament Facts

Do we really believe these promises for a deep inner, moral cleansing, or do we try to explain them away? Have our ears grown accustomed to those teachers who insist that Christians cannot live a single day without lusting, coveting, having evil thoughts, getting angry, causing dissension, committing immorality, lying and cheating, stealing and fornicating, committing adultery, worshiping mammon, and idolizing the forbidden? To listen to many of these well-intentioned writers and teachers—many whom are godly men and women—what God offers to the Christian under grace is no better than what the sinner had under the Law and bondage of sin. Where is the freedom from sin's bondage in such teaching? Where is the abundant life in such teaching? Where is there victory over temptation and sin in such teaching? Where is the power to love God with all one's heart, soul, mind and strength in such teaching?

Such teachers don't have the answer to these questions. They have explained away God's provision for such a deliverance and have reduced the biblical passages which address these issues to only goals to be sought, ideals never to be reached, and a reality left for the next world when one receives a glorified body. Some answers!

I like the answer that Baptist pastor A. J. Gordon (1836-1895) gave to those who said such teaching as the above was espousing unbiblical perfectionism: "In regard to the doctrine of sinless perfection as a heresy, we regard contentment with sinful imperfection as a greater heresy. And we gravely fear that many Christians make the apostle's words, 'If we say we have no sin we deceive ourselves,' the unconscious justification for a low standard of Christian living."[2] No, we don't advocate a "sinless perfectionism"; neither can we accept "sinful imperfectionism."

Jesus announced, "Blessed are the pure in heart, for they shall see God" (Matt. 5:8). Concerned about his vacillating converts, Paul wrote to the Corinthians: "I feel a divine jealousy for you, for I betrothed you to one husband, to present you as a pure virgin to Christ." (2 Cor. 11:2). The apostle's prayer-burden for his Philippian converts was: "And it is my prayer that . . . you may approve what is excellent, and so be pure and blameless for the day of Christ" (Phil. 1:9a-10). After charging Pastor Timothy with what the content of his teaching should consist of, Paul reminded him, "The aim of our charge is love that issues from a pure heart and a good conscience and a sincere faith" (1 Tim. 1:5). To the same man, Paul exhorted, "keep yourself pure" (1 Tim. 5:22b). The apostle reiterates the same moral admonition in his second letter to this first century pastor, and says that by complying with his apostolic commands Timothy will identify himself with the pure-hearted: "So flee youthful passions and pursue righteousness, faith, love, and peace, along with those who call on the Lord from a pure heart" (2 Tim. 2:22). To Elder Titus, the apostle mentions a category of Christians he identifies as "the pure": "To the pure, all things are pure, but to the defiled and unbelieving, nothing is pure; but both their minds and their consciences are defiled" (Titus 1:15). In 1 Peter 1:22, Peter exhorts the believers of his day to experience a greater degree of love for one another: "Having purified your souls by your obedience to the truth for a sincere brotherly love, love one another earnestly from a pure heart." Then, in testifying before the Jerusalem council as to what actually occurred among the Gentiles when he preached among them, the apostle Peter reported that Cornelius' household experienced substantially what the disciples themselves experienced on the day of Pentecost: "God, who knows the heart, bore witness to them, by giving them the Holy Spirit as he did to us, and he made no distinction between us and them, having cleansed their hearts by faith" (Acts 15:8-9).

In the above selected quotes on this subject of heart purity, the Lord Jesus spoke of those who "are the pure in heart"; Paul wrote to those he wanted to present some day as a "pure virgin to Christ"; and the same apostle prayed that his converts would be "pure . . . for the day of Christ." Paul also wrote about a "pure heart" and exhorted a pastor to live a sexually "pure" life. And Peter said the substantive essence of what occurred in the hearts of all who were present in the upper room on the day of Pentecost, as well as those present in Cornelius' house when Peter preached, was that their hearts were "cleansed . . . by faith." These, and the entirety of Scripture make clear to all who will see, that God promises a pure heart, that the apostles prayed for their converts to have a pure heart, that the Holy Spirit wrought a deep inner cleansing in the hearts of the 120 on the day of Pentecost, and that Jesus said it is the pure-hearted that "shall see God."

Not Sinless Perfection

To teach the biblical doctrine of heart-purity is not the same as espousing the erroneous teaching of *sinless* Christian perfection. The one is Christ-centered; the other man-centered. The one is totally reliant on Christ; the other exalts the will. The one walks in humility before an absolutely holy God; the other boasts of his righteousness and purity; the one freely acknowledges how far short of God's glory he falls; the other is incapable of admitting trespasses and failures in his love; the one lives at the foot of the Cross of Christ Jesus; the other is proud and self-righteous; the one's hope is in "nothing less than Jesus' blood and righteousness"; the other trusts in his good works, resolutions, and ecstatic experiences; the one is fully conscious that in *himself* he is altogether unrighteous, unholy, sinful, and defiled; the other boasts of his personal sanctity and enjoys showcasing his *Christian* maturity.

These two categories of believers are as different as the two men Jesus spoke of worshiping in the Temple. The one was guilty of comparing *his holiness* to those he viewed with contempt: "God, I thank you that I am not like other men — robbers, evildoers, adulterers — or even like this tax collector." The other knew that compared to God's holiness, *his* was nothing: "He would not even look up to heaven, but beat his breast and said, 'God, have mercy on me, a sinner.'" Which one caught the eye of Jesus? The latter: "I tell you that this man, rather than the other, went home justified before God. For everyone who exalts himself will be humbled, and he who humbles himself will be exalted" (Luke 18:9-14).

It is important to note this distinction between *sinless* Christian perfection and the biblical teaching of heart-purity, because too many Christians reject the biblical teaching for fear of accepting an unbiblical doctrine. However, we should not allow our fears of adopting the one to cause us to be prejudiced against exploring the other. God desires that his people experience more than the forgiveness of sins; he challenges them to trust him for a deep inner renewal, whereby there is a death to *self*ism and an infused fullness of the Spirit's energizing purity and power.

Pentecost

The pure heart the Lord Jesus and the apostles spoke of is a gift — a gift not unlike what was given on the day of Pentecost to each thirsty-hearted disciple. Where the Spirit comes in power and fullness, prepared hearts have been purified by the Spirit's fiery presence to a degree that was not experienced in regenerating grace. Peter is a prime example.

The founder of the Christian & Missionary Alliance, Dr. A. B. Simpson, came to discover the reality of this truth while pastoring a Presbyterian church in Louisville, Kentucky many years ago. Speaking of Peter and all who were filled with the Spirit at Pentecost, Simpson wrote,

> The change produced by the baptism of the Holy Spirit upon the first disciples was more remarkable in their own lives than even in their service and testimony.
>
> Peter was the irresolute disciple — always running ahead of his Master. Boasting in his self-confidence of what he would do or would not do, yet he ran away at the threat of a servant girl. The power of the Spirit transformed him into the fearless hero who stood before the murderers of his Lord and charged them with their crime. With lowly spirit and humble heart, Peter went forth to walk in his Master's steps, and at last to die upon his Master's cross with downward head. The miracle in Peter's personal life is greater than the wondrous power of his public testimony. Nothing is so strong as the influence of a consistent, supernatural, and holy character.[3]

English Methodism's Samuel Chadwick (1860-1932), in writing about the impact of the Spirit as "the Spirit of fire" upon ministers of the Word, observed, "Pentecost transforms the preacher. The commonest bush ablaze with the presence of God becomes a miracle of glory."[3] Fire energizes; fire purifies. Pentecost energizes; Pentecost purifies. The Holy Spirit energizes; the Holy Spirit purifies. In the words of Chadwick: "Suppose we try Pentecost!"[4]

The God Who is Able

Could we now ask the Spirit of God to search our hearts? Let us ask: Have I fallen into the ground and *died* to self? Am I existentially *crucified* with Christ? Am I living to please myself, or the Lord? Can I say with Peter that God has cleansed my heart by faith? Am I totally the Lord's?

Dear reader, if God can keep a coal miner's eyes clean from coal dust, don't you think the same God can purify and keep your heart clean as you walk through a filthy world?

A kingdom of righteousness and love
*   has marched in with my King from above;*
Overthrowing every native foe,
*   breaking down heavily entrenched woe.*
His campaign perseveres without end,
*   taking forces reluctant to bend.*
Christ reigns within!

The kingdom of God has come inside;
*   my heart, the King, has come to reside.*
The standard He's raised is holiness;
*   his Name will settle for nothing less.*
With merciful grace He shapes my will,
*   breathing His power in me to fill.*
Christ reigns within!

CHAPTER 8

The Pure in Heart
(Part 3)

In Part 1 of this series, I cited a few Old Testament promises that pointed to a coming day in which God said he would purify seeking hearts:

> "I will sprinkle clean water on you and you shall be clean from all your uncleanness, and from all your idols I will cleanse you" (Ezk 36:25).[1]

> "Many will be purified, made spotless and refined" (Dan. 12:10 NIV).

> "For he is like a refiner's fire and like a fuller's soap. He will sit as a refiner and purifier of silver, and he will purify the sons of Levi and refine them like gold and silver, and they will bring offerings of righteousness to the LORD" (Mal. 3:2-3).

In parts 1 and 2, I cited several New Testament texts which emphasize heart purity. For example, "Blessed are the pure in heart for they shall see God" (Matt. 5:8). "The aim of our charge is love that issues from a pure heart and a good conscience and a sincere faith" (1 Tim. 1:5). "Having purified your souls by your obedience to the truth for a sincere brotherly love, love one another earnestly from a pure heart" (1 Pet. 1:22).

I also noted that heart purity is not to be confused with sinless perfection; it is a gift of God to be experientially realized in this life to the praise of the Lord Jesus Christ.

Now, let's proceed further.

The *Heart* of the Matter

The heart of the human personality is that inner faculty of man where one's thoughts and imaginations, desires and aspirations, and choices and actions originate. It is the very fountainhead and spring from which all man's attitudes and behavior flow.

Christianity is a religion of the *heart*. True, it is a way of life, but it is a way of life that flows from the heart.

When the Lord Jesus Christ enters a person's life, he enters the very heart of that person to set up his kingdom, and from there launches a campaign to bring under his sovereign reign every facet of man's life.

Man-made, self-righteous religion expends enormous will power to conform one's life to a self-devised code of religious conduct. Such religion is merely externalized futility, which ends in disillusionment and despair. After all, "Can the Ethiopian change his skin or the leopard his spots" (Jer. 13:23)?

The Heart Impacts Our Conversation

During his earthly life and ministry, the Lord Jesus always went to the *heart* of the matter. Jesus said even one's conversation is heart-revealing.

Addressing hypocritical Pharisees one day, Jesus intuitively knew these religious pretenders were evil people. While projecting an image of goodness, Jesus knew they were corrupt at the core. Christ called them a nest of snakes — a "brood of vipers," saying, "Either make the tree good and its fruit good, or make the tree bad and its fruit bad, for the tree is known by its fruit. You brood of vipers! How can you speak good, when you are evil? For out of the abundance of the heart the mouth speaks. The good person out of his good treasure brings forth good, and the evil person out of his evil treasure brings forth evil" (Matt. 12:33-35).

Jesus said of these people that it was impossible for them to pursue a lifestyle of wholesome conversation with others because of the condition of their hearts. The tree was "bad," therefore it produced bad fruit.

The apostle Paul exhorted believers of his day, "Let there be no filthiness nor foolish talk nor crude joking, which are out of place . . ." (Eph. 5:4). Christians don't tell off-colored jokes. Christians don't use profanities, vulgarities, obscenities, or hang around people who do (if they can help it). Christians don't share salacious stories, or laugh at those who do. Why is this? Because their once defiled hearts have been purified. And purified hearts—hearts enthroned by the pure Christ—do not use their consecrated tongues for filthy purposes.

Now, lest Satan should take advantage of a recent convert, allow me to provide this note of caution. The old language—the language of "Egypt"—may not necessarily leave overnight, but it *will* leave.

E. Stanley Jones, who served Christ in India for more than fifty years, speaks to this point from personal experience. He said the next morning following his conversion, "I walked out into a new world. The trees seemed to clap their hands; the sky was never so blue, and nature was never so alive and radiant." Jones said he was feeling so good, "I walked up to my chum, Ras, slapped him on the back, and said, 'My, what a d___ fine day!" Jones amusingly adds, "The angels must have smiled and said: 'He's trying to say "Hallelujah," but he doesn't know the language yet.' "[2]

But Paul not only said what God's people should *not* speak with their tongues, but what they should use their tongues for: "but instead let there be thanksgiving" (Eph. 5:4). Let there be continuous thanksgiving to God from the lips of Christians. "I thank you, Father" (Matt. 11:25) characterized the life of Jesus. It did the same in the life of Paul; so it should for us. It will if the heart is good and pure.

The Heart Impacts Our Conduct

One cannot be a disciple of the Lord Jesus Christ and live a filthy life. It's absolutely impossible! How is that? Because a disciple of Christ is indwelt by the *Holy* Spirit. And where the Holy Spirit dwells he brings with him divine holiness, a divine purity—the very purity of the ascended Christ.

Where the Holy Spirit does not have control, the religious man and woman will do their best to conform to a man-made standard of purity and righteousness. Such people *major* on externals and *minor* on heart matters. Such were the Pharisees of Jesus' day who were fanatical regarding their dietary laws, for example. To these people, Jesus said, "There is nothing outside a person that by going into him can defile him [I can almost hear one of them choke on his broccoli at this point!], but the things that come out of a person are what defile them" (Mark. 7:15).

Christ's own disciples needed him to interpret what he meant by this saying. Jesus explained, "What comes out of a person is what defiles him. For from within, out of the heart of man, come evil thoughts, sexual immorality, theft, murder, adultery, coveting, wickedness, deceit, sensuality, envy, slander, pride, foolishness. All these evil things come from within, and they defile a person" (Mark. 7:20-23).

Why is sexual immorality so pervasive in our culture? Because of impure hearts. Why is plagiarism so wide-spread in our educational institutions? Because of impure hearts. Why do applicants lie and embellish their résumés? Because of impure hearts. Why do marriages too often end in divorce? Because of impure hearts. Why are we so discontent with what we have? Because of impure hearts. Why is there so much bickering and complaining in some homes? Because of impure hearts. Why do we indulge our eyes with risqué media? Because of impure hearts. Why do we criticize our brothers and sisters in Christ, thus exalting ourselves? Because of impure hearts. Why do some women wear immodest necklines and hemlines? Because of impure hearts. Why is it easier for us to think bad of a person instead of good? Because of impure hearts. Why do we insist on having our own way in church business meetings? Because of impure hearts. Why do we run from church to church, trying to find the perfect one? Because of impure hearts.

Those Who Received Pure Hearts

I realize there are those Bible scholars and teachers who say a pure heart is beyond our "wildest dreams" in this life and none should expect to receive such. Interesting, isn't it? These religious sophists apparently believe themselves to be wiser than the Scriptures, for the Lord Jesus and the apostles taught that God wants all of his children to enjoy a pure heart and, furthermore, the Scriptures record that many did.

Peter says he and the 120 disciples received pure hearts on the day of Pentecost, and that a man by the name of Cornelius did also along with his entire household. Testifying at the first Jerusalem Council, having been convened for the purpose of giving Paul and Barnabas an opportunity to explain their ministry among the Gentiles, Peter defends Paul's ministry by explaining what happened when he himself first preached among Gentiles. Peter stood to his feet and reminded the church leaders how God had sent him to preach the gospel among Gentiles: "God, who knows the heart, bore witness to them, by giving them the Holy Spirit just as he did to us, and he made no distinction between us and them, having cleansed their hearts by faith" (Acts 15:8-9). A cleansed heart is a pure heart. You cannot have a pure heart without having a cleansed heart.

This same apostle Peter, the apostle who had received a pure heart along with all the other disciples on the day of Pentecost, wrote years later to first-century Christians: "Having purified your souls by your obedience to the truth for a sincere brotherly love, love one another earnestly from a pure heart" (1 Pet. 1:22).

The issue here is not some theory of sanctification as to how one may receive a pure heart. The question should be, *Do I have a pure heart?* You say, "I'm clothed with the righteousness of Christ." Does such a doctrine purify your heart? You say, "Christ's righteousness has been imputed to my account." Does such a belief give you a pure heart? Theories won't change the heart. I don't merely need a theory of righteousness or sanctification. I need a pure heart. It is not a question of what Augustine, Luther, or Wesley said about the matter. It is a question of whether I will receive what God has promised, what Christ has provided through his death and resurrection, and what the Holy Spirit effectually makes real to all thirsty hearts. We don't need more theories of righteousness and sanctification. We need more God-thirsty men and women who will do what young Donald McPhail did one morning.

The Scottish Presbyterian revivalist Duncan Campbell (1898-

1972), used to tell the story about a young man who came to Christ during the mighty move of the Spirit in the Hebrides Islands in the 1950s. Donald McPhail was his name. Some time following his conversion, Donald was sorely struggling with his divided heart. On the one hand, he was rejoicing over his new-found Savior; on the other hand, he was debating whether he should truly be Christ's disciple by surrendering his all.

One morning, according to his established ritual, he went out to a hillside to pray. Donald knew little about the Bible or theology. He was merely hungering and thirsting after the righteousness of God. He wanted to be *one* with God. In great agony of prayer he cried that day, "Lord Jesus, if you don't do something for me soon, I can't take it any more!"

Donald would later confide to Duncan Campbell that God heard his prayer, giving him a cleansing unlike any he had known before, and uniting a previously divided heart.

It seems to me there are at least three cleansings spoken of in the New Testament. These cleansings are grounded in the atoning sacrifice and resurrection of Christ and effected by the Holy Spirit. No one should ever speak of his own sanctity, but neither should he deny the power of God to do in him what Christ died for and for which the Holy Spirit was sent.

1. There is the cleansing of the conscience from the guilt of sins committed. Note these examples:

> [L]et us draw near with a true heart in full assurance of faith, with our hearts sprinkled clean from an evil conscience and our bodies washed with pure water (Heb. 10:22).

> If we confess our sins, he is faithful and just to forgive us our sins and to cleanse us from all unrighteousness (1 John 1:9).

2. There is a cleansing of the heart from the defilement of sin.

"I baptize you with water for repentance, but he who is coming after me is mightier than I, whose sandals I am not worthy to carry. He will baptize you with the Holy Spirit and fire. 12 His winnowing fork is in his hand, and he will clear his threshing floor and gather his wheat into the barn, but the chaff he will burn with unquenchable fire" (Matt. 3:11-12).

". . . and he made no distinction between us and them, having cleansed their hearts by faith (Acts 15:9).

3. There is a daily, continuous cleansing available and necessary for all God's children.

Jesus said to him, "The one who has bathed does not need to wash, except for his feet, but is completely clean. And you are clean, but not every one of you." (John 13:10).

But if we walk in the light, as he is in the light, we have fellowship with one another, and the blood of Jesus his Son cleanses us from all sin (1 John 1:7).

I now ask you, Would the Lord Jesus have told us, "Blessed are the pure in heart, for they shall see God," if he could not give the thirsty-hearted a pure heart? Would Peter have declared that the hearts of Cornelius' household and those of the 120 were purified on the day of Pentecost if they were not? Would Peter later have exhorted Christians to love one another with a pure heart if such a heart condition were unavailable in this life?

Let's not preoccupy ourselves with *theories* of sanctification. Let's go to the High Priest himself, asking him to satisfy our heart's need. If you do so, I believe you will discover that through the shed blood of Christ and the fiery ministry of the Holy Spirit, he will give you a heart as pure as he gave to Peter and many others. After all, isn't that one of our fundamental needs? "Now to him who is able to do far more abundantly than all that we ask or think, according to the power at work within us, . . ." (Eph. 3:20).

I need more than my sins forgiven, O Lord;

My heart is divided and unclean.
Excise all that contaminates the wellspring,
Uniting my heart, making it clean.

I need more than my sins forgiven, O Lord;
My heart is raging at war within.
Come, mighty Conqueror, Flame of holy love,
Removing every stain of sin.

CHAPTER 9

The Pure in Heart
(Part 4)

I concluded Part 3 of this series by making three brief observations on this subject of heart purity:

- There is a cleansing of the conscience from the guilt of sins committed.
- There is a cleansing of the heart from the defilement of sin acquired.
- There is a daily cleansing available and necessary for all God's children.

Let's take a closer look.

Examination

The Bible teaches that there is the cleansing of the heart/conscience from the guilt of sins committed and the defilement of sin acquired. While the New Testament has a great deal to say on this subject, I want to examine one text in particular.

Hebrews 10:22 draws a connection between conscience and cleansing, the heart and cleansing: "Let us draw near with a true heart in full assurance of faith, with our hearts sprinkled clean from an evil conscience and our bodies washed with pure water" (Heb. 10:22).[1]

This text is located following an extensive delineation by the writer of the efficacious superiority of Christ's atoning sacrifice and priesthood. Any careful student of the Bible will note a carryover in this text of Old Testament concepts and language (this shouldn't surprise us since throughout this epistle he takes for granted the readers' familiarity with the Jewish sacrificial system). The writer is informing his New Covenant readers how one is to approach God, and he says one of the essential components to approaching God properly is to have "our hearts sprinkled clean from an evil conscience." What does he mean by this? Let's look at the keys words in this text.

"hearts"

"Heart," as used metaphorically in the Bible, refers to man's inner being. It is the fountainhead and faculty of one's emotions, motives, aspirations, thoughts, attitudes, and will. The New Testament identifies a wide assortment of heart conditions. For example, it speaks of hearts that are pure, dull, good, evil, hard, distant from God, doubting, honest, and so forth (See, for example, Matt. 5:8; 13:15; 15:8; 19:8; Mark 3:5; 11:23).

"sprinkled"

The term "sprinkled," and its cognates, are used in the Old Testament in connection with the Tabernacle/Temple worship system. Under this system, there were three physical properties employed by the priests which were applied to various objects by the mode of *sprinkling*: blood, water, and oil. Two of these properties — blood and water — were designated by God to represent *cleansing* from sin.

In the book of Leviticus, there are at least four specific occasions in which God directed the priests to sprinkle sacrificial blood in order to make an atonement for sin.

First: Blood was to be sprinkled whenever any unintentional sin was committed by an individual or a group (see Lev. 4). After the individual or group became aware of their sin, they were to offer the prescribed offering. Blood from a bull was to be sprinkled seven times before the veil by a priest, with a portion of the same blood applied to the four horns of the altar of incense. The result? "And the priest shall make atonement for them, and they shall be forgiven" (Lev. 4:20, 26, 31, 35).

Second: In Leviticus 5 there are a number of sins listed which require blood atonement. When the transgressor "realizes his guilt in any of these and confesses the sin he has committed, he shall bring to the LORD as his guilt penalty for the sin that he has committed, . . ." Lev. 5:5-6). The priest then takes the blood and sprinkles some of it on the side of the altar of sacrifice (5:9). The result? "And the priest shall make atonement for him for the sin that he has committed, and he shall be forgiven" (5:10).

Third: Leviticus 14 contains specific laws for the ceremonial cleansing of lepers. While there was no inherent moral evil in the disease of leprosy,[2] it seems that this disease was used by God to *typify* moral liability for acquired sin. Otherwise, why would a guilt/sin offering be required? After a person was healed from this disease of leprosy, blood from a sacrificial bird was to be sprinkled seven times on the person as a sign of cleansing, after which he bathed in clean water. On the eighth day of the cleansing ritual, blood was taken from the guilt offering (a male lamb) and applied to the right ear, right thumb, and big right toe of the cured leper. The same was to be done with ceremonial oil. The result? "Thus the priest shall make atonement for him, and he shall be clean" (Lev. 14:20).

Fourth: Leviticus 16 recounts a variety of rituals surrounding the Day of Atonement (*Yom Kippur*). The symbolism of the day was pronounced. Aaron, the high priest, offered a bull as a sacrificial atonement for his personal sins and those of his family. Then God said, "he shall take some of the blood of the bull and sprinkle it with his finger on the front of the mercy seat on the east side, and in front of the mercy seat he shall sprinkle some of the blood with his finger seven times (Leviticus 16:14).

Next, Aaron brought the blood of a goat as a sin offering inside the veil and sprinkled it over and in front of the mercy seat. Afterward, he sprinkled the blood of the bull and goat on the horns of the brazen altar, consecrating it "for the uncleannesses of the people of Israel" (Lev. 16:19).

"clean"

This word does not appear in the original text but is implied. Acknowledging this, the *New American Standard Bible* italicizes supplied words, of which this is one. The reason some Bible versions have supplied the word "clean" in this text is because the concept of "sprinkling" suggests cleansing—either ritual or moral cleansing, depending on the context.

The concept of the sprinkling atoning blood in the Old Testament always suggested the idea of the forgiveness, removal, and cleansing of sin. Whoever had acquired guilt and defilement as a result of sin, were pronounced clean following the necessary confession and prescribed atonement.

"evil"

Evil is the opposite of morally good. A person or act is either morally good or bad according to God's predetermined standard of goodness. The word "evil" (*ponēros*) occurs in the Greek text a total of seventy-eight times in the New Testament. The Bible speaks of an evil heart, evil thoughts, evil people, evil culture, evil conduct, evil speech, evil conscience, and so forth (See, for example, Matt. 5:8; 13:15; 15:8; 19:8; Mark 3:5; 11:23).

"Conscience"

The conscience is that God-given moral faculty whereby one is able to discern the difference between right and wrong, good and evil. It can only be safely trusted as a guide in making moral decisions to the degree it is informed by the Word of God and controlled by the Holy Spirit (see, for example, Rom. 9:1).

The word "conscience" (Greek: *syneidēsis*) occurs some twenty-seven times in the New Testament; the writers speak of a variety of consciences: good, clear, weak, wounded, seared, defiled, imperfect, pure, and evil (See, for example, Acts 23:1; Acts 24:16; 1 Cor. 8:10, 12; 1 Tim. 4:2; Titus 1:15; Heb. 9:9, 14; 10:22.

Interpretation

As I have previously noted, Hebrews 10:22—and the entire book, for that matter—can only be understood in view of the Old Testament, and in particular the book of Leviticus.

God directed Moses to institute a variety of religious rituals involving animal sacrifices. As a part of the atonement ritual in some of these sacrifices, blood was to be sprinkled either/or in front of the veil, on the altar of incense and sacrifice, on the confessor, in front of the mercy seat, and on a defiled house.

Following the sprinkling of the blood, those who had either committed unintentional sins or known sins, were declared absolved, forgiven of all incurred guilt. They were cleansed from sin. In the case of those who had contracted leprosy and were subsequently cured, these were pronounced clean by the priest after undergoing a series of rituals. In the case of the Day of Atonement, individuals were not required to present their own sacrifice for atonement; sacrifices were offered by the high priest for all the sins for all the people, thus making atonement.

Now we know there was no inherent moral righteousness in a sacrificial bull, goat, lamb, or dove—"For it is impossible for the blood of bulls and goats to take away sins" (Heb. 10:4)—these served as antitypes of the perfect sacrifice to come. Although the Old Covenant believer was indeed forgiven and justified by God, the remedy for sin and the existential reality of forgiveness and cleansing were incomplete.

The late British New Testament scholar F. F. Bruce (1910-1990) remarks on this: "The sin-offerings presented on the Day of Atonement, or at any other time, had no effect on the consciences of those on whose behalf they were brought; they served merely in an external and symbolical manner to counteract the defilement of sin."[2] The author of Hebrews summarized this truth in the following words: "According to this arrangement, gifts and sacrifices are offered that cannot perfect the conscience of the worshiper, but deal only with food and drink and various washings, regulations for the body imposed until the time of reformation (Heb. 9:9-10).

But there is Good News! What Aaron and all his successors never perfected under the Law; what the millions of gallons of blood shed on the Tabernacle/Temple altar and sprinkled before the veil and mercy seat could never achieve with any finality—the one perfect offering by the Lord Jesus Christ did: "For if the sprinkling of defiled persons with the blood of goats and bulls and with the ashes of a heifer sanctifies for the purification of the flesh, how much more will the blood of Christ, who through the eternal Spirit offered himself without blemish to God, purify our conscience from dead works to serve the living God" (Hebrews 9:14). Isaac Watts (1674-1748) movingly captured this truth in the following words:

Not all the blood of beasts
On Jewish altars slain
Could give the guilty conscience peace
Or wash away the stain.

But Christ, the heav'nly Lamb,
Takes all our sins away;
A sacrifice of nobler name
And richer blood than they.[3]

Appropriation

What God through Christ accomplished once-for-all by the atoning death of his Son on the cross, is now to be appropriated by faith by all repentant seekers. The shed blood of Christ is both efficacious for the forgiveness of sins committed and the defilement of sin acquired. The blood of Christ—wonder of wonders—removes both the record of sin against the sinner and the pollution of sin defiling the conscience. When the heart has been *sprinkled* clean by appropriating Christ himself, an evil conscience gives way to a clean conscience. Where there is a clean heart there is a clean conscience.

Because the heart has been cleansed of all moral contaminants, the conscience is now able to function as God intended it to. As it is continually informed by the Word of God and led by the Spirit of God, the conscience will remain pure and clean. Whenever it fails to act in harmony with God's truth, it becomes tainted and is in need of cleansing. Immediate repentance assures immediate cleansing; delayed obedience results in delayed cleansing. If we desire our hearts to be kept clean before God, we must live a life of conscious reliance on Christ, our ascended, mediating High Priest. Christ is faithfully fulfilling his part to keep us safe and clean; we must do our part to walk in obedience before him: "But if we walk in the light, as he is in the light, we have fellowship with one another, and the blood of Jesus his Son cleanses us from all sin" (1 John 1:7) — sins acquired as well as the infection of sin. Sin in every form and description, sin in every act and condition have no power to withstand the cleansing blood of Christ.

Dear reader, take heart. Embrace the sprinkled blood of Christ and be clean!

Again, Isaac Watts:

My faith would lay her hand
On that dear head of Thine,
While, like a penitent, I stand,
And there confess my sin.

Believing, we rejoice
To see the curse remove;
We bless the Lamb with cheerful voice,
And sing His bleeding love.[4]

CHAPTER 10

The Crucified Life

At the very heart of Christianity there stands a Cross. Apart from the atoning, vicarious death of Jesus Christ for the world's sin, Christianity is reduced to an empty philosophy at its best or a cult at its worst. But this Cross-event was different because of who hung there: God's unique Son.

The sovereign God and Creator of the universe gave up to that Cross his only begotten Son for man's redemption and salvation. When God's Lamb cried out that horrible and wonderful day, "It is finished!", the way to God had been completed because there was now at last a sacrifice that was perfect: the sinless Son of God.

As the Cross is central to the Christian faith, so it is central to the Christian life. Just as there could be no salvation for man without the Cross of Christ and an empty Tomb, there can be no victory in the Christian's walk apart from the Cross.

The Cross means death! When Jesus Christ died on Calvary's Cross, he was not the only one who died — he took our old *self* with him and nailed it to the tree! It is an objective fact of that salvation-event that a death-blow was struck to the old *self*: "We know that our old self was crucified with him in order that the body of sin might be brought to nothing, so that we would no longer be enslaved to sin" (Rom. 6:6).

Now because of this, here is a beautiful fact and an open secret revealed to all of God's hungry-hearted seekers: Christian, you need not live a defeated life; your old *self* was crucified on the Cross of Christ!

Oh, how many Christians there are who have languished in a spiritual wasteland since the day of their conversion to Jesus Christ. They have been born again, but they have no consistent victory over sin. They know their name is written down in the Lamb's Book of Life, but their walk with God is punctuated with two steps forward and one step backward — or is that vice versa?

Thank God, our sins have all been forgiven through Christ, but now what? How many of us, following our conversion to Christ, can identify with this English lad, who some six months after he placed his trust in Jesus Christ as his Lord and Savior, he went to a little hillside with a very troubled heart to talk with God. He cried, "Lord Jesus, if this is all you can do for me, I can't take it anymore!" He had no more than prayed that prayer when the Lord Jesus whom he had addressed revealed to Donald MacPhail by his Spirit, that he had not only died for his sins, but had nailed his sinful *self* to the Cross as well. The young man left the hillside that day empowered with a new level of real spiritual knowledge: not only were his sins forgiven, but his sinful *self* was crucified on the Cross as well.

The truth of this reality is what the apostle Paul wrote about in Romans 6. He was writing to those who had come to faith in Christ but were failing to possess their possessions. Their conduct too often was characterized by failure and defeat instead of victory. They were *failing* Christians. What is God's answer for the defeated Christian? Is there a word from Heaven? Yes, there is; it's found in Romans 6 (as well as other texts). Rejoice with me in this truth.

Remember what took place on the Cross of Christ. "We know that our old self was crucified with him in order that the body of sin might be brought to nothing, so that we would no longer be enslaved to sin" (Rom. 6:6).

Why is it so imperative for Christians to *know* this? Because "one who has died has been set free from sin" (Rom. 6:7). No, Paul isn't advocating a kind of cultic sinless perfectionism. He is simply stating a glorious reality: In the death of Christ we have also died, and since we have died in his death we have been delivered — freed from the tyranny of sin.

This is *the* answer for every defeated Christian. Struggling believer, the gospel is Good News for the Christian as well as for the sinner. All of your defeats and failures have been nailed to the Cross of Christ. Your victory has been already won and secured for you through the Cross. You don't need to *live* in defeat! Do I now hear some skeptical believer sighing, "So what! What can I do about it?" Here's what God tells us to do.

Take a step of courageous faith: "So you also must consider yourselves dead to sin and alive to God in Christ Jesus (Rom. 6:11). Paul is saying that what happened as historical fact on the cross of Christ, must now be appropriated through faith. This will involve on our part, a total surrender to the lordship of Jesus Christ and a full consecration of our body to God (review the remainder of Romans 6-8). But I assure you, on the authority of God's Word, if you allow the Holy Spirit to help you appropriate this truth in your own life, you will discover a dimension in your walk with God that is both deeper and higher than you ever thought possible. What you had come to believe was the *normal* Christian life — defeat and despair — will now be left behind for a Canaan Land of growth, real spiritual knowledge and fruitfulness through abiding in the Vine, the Lord Jesus Christ. "Now to him who is able to do far more abundantly than all that we ask or think, according to the power at work within us . . ." (Eph. 3:20).

I must confess that I wish I had known this truth and experienced the reality of it years before I did. If I had been more sensitive to the Holy Spirit, undoubtedly I would not have languished so long. This crucifixion of the old *self* on the Cross of Christ, and its consequent appropriation in our own life, is what Paul testifies to in Galatians 2:20 NASB: "I have been crucified with Christ; and it is no longer I who live, but Christ lives in me; and the life which I now live in the flesh I live by faith in the Son of God, who loved me and gave himself up for me."

What glorious freedom and reality! Paul says that the old "I" is nailed to the Cross; the old "I" no longer shares the throne of its heart with Christ. It is all Christ's. Christ has set up his kingdom in his heart and the old self, the old *ego,* the old "I" has been dethroned and rendered powerless. Friend, is this so in your life? Have you discovered the open secret of the crucified life in Christ? If you have, and have entered into the reality of the crucified life with the Lord Jesus Christ, I know you are making some exciting new discoveries. Let's note a few.

You have discovered that you don't need to be great or to be first. The need to be first and to be great is a common affliction for those Christians who are *not* walking the crucified road. You remember the disciples argument about this matter, don't you? "on the way they had argued with one another about who was the greatest. 35 And he sat down and called the twelve. And he said to them, 'If anyone would be first, he must be last of all and servant of all'" (Mark 9:34-35).

Christ rebuked the disciples sharply for playing this vain game of comparisons. And this was happening in Christ's own inner circle — in the Church. My wife and I often remark in our travels about those churches with "First" in their names. First, First, First! That's humble of them, isn't it? Even in the selection of the name of our own church identity, we resort to fleshly ecclesiastical comparisons. We were here *first!* Well, a crucified person soon discovers that he and she doesn't have to be first.

You have discovered that you don't need everyone's approval. That's not to imply that you don't appreciate the sincere affirmations of significant others in your life. You should, and do, I'm sure. And the longer I live the more I value the expressed appreciation and wisdom that comes from the body of Christ. There's rarely a week that goes by that I don't receive an expression of appreciation from a brother or sister in the Lord. I'm so grateful for their taking the time to call or write, or voicing their approval to me one-on-one. But those who walk the crucified road don't live out the will of God with the overriding thought of, "What will they think?" "Will they approve of this?" There were those in Jesus' day who were afraid to confess Christ openly. Why? Jesus said it was because "they loved the glory that comes from man more than the glory that comes from God" (John 12:43).

The church needs men and women who are fearless in their walk with God. The church needs pastors and church leaders who fear God more than the faces of men. The crucified man and woman walks with an eye that is single to the glory and praise of God. We don't seek approval from others, and we don't live in fear of others' disapproval. The crucified man will seek to do the will of God — regardless.

You have discovered that you don't need to have the last word. We are not the final word and we don't need to be the last word. Christ is the final Word — he's the Amen!

How many church conflicts, tensions, and splits could have been avoided if only . . . if only we had spoken with humility. If only we had deferred to our brothers and sisters in Christ in issues of moral indifference. If only we had kept quiet. If only we had heard wisdom coming from our brother's mouth instead of our own. We need to remember that no matter how long we have served the Lord, we can still *step off* from the crucified road. Holiness and humility are always found in the company of each another; where you find the one, the other will be close by.

Dallas Willard (1935-2013) was a university philosophy professor for many years. During one of his class sessions, a student took issue with Willard over a position he had stated. In doing so, the student was both disrespectful and obnoxious toward Willard. Sharing this incident later with a minister friend, his friend asked Willard why he hadn't responded to the student. Willard replied, "Because I was practicing the discipline of not having to have the *last* word."

You have discovered that you're not perfect. Oh, some would say that they already knew that before. Really? No man or woman knows in truth how limited and imperfect he is until he has gazed into the face of the crucified, sinless Son of God. Once we have caught a glimpse of him and start down the crucified road, keeping our eyes fixed on Jesus, how we view ourselves is totally different. Then we can readily say, "I'm sorry"; "I don't know"; "You were right"; "I didn't realize that"; "I apologize"; "Please forgive me."

Even the great Apostle Paul apologized once he discovered he was in error. Standing before the Sanhedrin Council to give an account of his witness to Christ and his resurrection, he announced to the Jewish leaders that he had lived with a "good conscience up to this day." Whereupon, Ananias the high priest ordered Paul to strike him. Paul's immediate response? "God is going to strike you, you whitewashed wall! Are you sitting to judge me according to the law, and yet contrary to the law you order me to be struck?" Paul was immediately rebuked by certain men: "Would you revile God's high priest?" And what did Paul do? Did he defend himself? No, because he was in the wrong; he had spoken disrespectfully of God's duly appointed leader. With humility the apostle apologized: "I did not know, brothers, that he was the high priest, for it is written, 'You shall not speak evil of a ruler of your people'" (see Acts 23:1-5).

You have discovered the abiding life. Along with many of God's children, you have discovered that the key to living an abundant life in Christ is to abide in Christ (see John 15). You have learned that as wonderful as certain spiritual experiences may be along this crucified road, the most critical thing for you to do is to simply trust and obey our Lord in whatever area of your life he chooses to address.

Because you cherish an uninterrupted fellowship with your Lord more than life itself, you will make any sacrifice, pay any price, and go to any length in order to keep his smile upon you. You want to keep his commandments and always do those things that are pleasing in his sight. And when you have discovered that you have grieved the Holy Spirit about a matter, you will leave no stone unturned until Canaan's music is singing sweetly in your heart once again.

I know there are a multitude of other discoveries you have made as well. What is the secret latch that unlocks the door to this crucified life? Hear the words of our Lord:

> "Truly, truly, I say to you, unless a grain of wheat falls into the earth and dies, it remains alone; but if it dies, it bears much fruit. He who loves his life loses it, and he who hates his life in this world will keep it to life eternal. If anyone serves Me, he must follow Me; and where I am, there My servant will be also; if anyone serves Me, the Father will hon-

or him" (John 12:24-26 NASB).

Appropriate this life—the crucified life, Christ's life—and live a blessed life!

I have been crucified with Christ,
  nailed to the Cross was I —

  the I twisted inward,
  the I blinded outward,

  the I driven to succeed,
  the I grasping with greed,

  the I never in wrong,
  the I with no true song,

  the I self-directed,
  the I self-affected.

I have been crucified with Christ,
  nevertheless I live —

  not the old I resides,
  for Christ in me abides.

I have been crucified with Christ,
  and the life I now live I . . .

  live by faith in the Son,
  by whose love I've been won,

  who defeated the I
  when He gave his last cry.

CHAPTER 11

The Risen Life

For many years Northern Ireland experienced great political turmoil. At one time, among the revolutionary slogans painted on the walls of buildings in Belfast was this one, "Beware of risen people!"

While the author of this piece of graffiti had in mind underground Irish revolutionaries, the slogan fittingly identifies another breed of "risen" people—Christians who have been brought to life through the resurrecting power of the Lord Jesus Christ. Just as every believer who has trusted in Jesus Christ as Lord and Savior was taken to the Cross with him and died to sin in his death (see previous chapter), so every believer was raised with Christ when he strode from the empty tomb that early Lord's Day morning. Hallelujah!

Among the early followers of Christ, the Apostle Paul in particular was given a special insight into the implications of the believer's own position and identity in the death and resurrection of the Lord Jesus.

The Bible affirms that in Christ's death our old *self was* crucified with him (Rom. see 6:6); it also affirms that the believer is united with Christ through his resurrection life (see Rom. 6:5). It is through the gift of faith that the repentant sinner appropriates the provisions of the Cross and the Empty Tomb. When that takes place, the guilty, condemned sinner receives God's pardoning grace, is justified freely, given new life in Christ, and has been set apart to God from sin to live only for God.

Let's observe some of the practical and ethical implications of having been raised up with Christ. You say that you have been born again? That's great, but now what? How are you to live? How are you to behave? What does a real Christian look like? As we should expect, God has the answers for us in his Word. Let's take a look at Colossians 3.

A Christian Mindset

Paul says to recently converted persons, "If then you have been raised with Christ, seek the things that are above, where Christ is, seated at the right hand of God. 2 Set your minds on things that are above, not on things that are on earth. 3 For you have died, and your life is hidden with Christ in God" (Col. 3:1-3).[1]

By a power not his own, into the heart of the new Christian enters the Holy Spirit, who begins an intimate journey of jealously supervising the newborn child of God. One of the ministries of the Holy Spirit is to strengthen the will of the believer. He helps us to keep our focus where it should be. The apostle says the Christian is to "seek" and to "set." He and she is to seek "things above" and set the mind on "things above." The grammatical tenses and moods suggest that the Christian is to be always actively engaged in elevating his spiritual sight and intently keeping his mind centered on spiritual realities. Lest we wonder where the object of this mindset is, God does not leave us in the dark: "where Christ is seated at the right hand of God."

What are these lofty "things" the Christian is to seek and to set his mind on—these things that are found in Jesus Christ at God's right hand? As is so often the case in studying and meditating on God's Word, we see that the immediate context provides the answers. All the graces necessary to the believer to live a productive and God-glorifying life are found in Jesus Christ. What are some of these graces, which Paul calls "things above," that the believer is to seek? Let's take a look at verse 12.

A Compassionate Heart

It was Dr. Bob Pierce (1914-1978), founder of the *World Vision* humanitarian agency, who used to say often, "Let my heart break with the things that break the heart of God." That's a compassionate heart. We won't get a heart like that from drinking at this world's well of selfishness and hardness.

Fanny Crosby (1820-1915), the blind hymn writer of another generation, who was a things-above-seeker, had it right when she wrote,

Down in the human heart, crushed by the tempter,
Feelings lie buried that grace can restore;
Touched by a loving heart, wakened by kindness,
Chords that are broken will vibrate once more.[2]

Crosby could pen those words because she was highly familiar with the transforming impact of a compassionate heart. With a compassionate heart the Christian will be moved by the spiritual lostness of the crowd, the hunger and pain of humanity, and the sorrow of others. How the church needs this grace. How I need this grace. It's found in Christ, at God's right hand.

The Lord Jesus is the Christian's perfect example of what it means to not only *feel* compassion toward another, but to be *moved* with compassion. Over and over in the Gospel accounts, Jesus was moved to act when he felt compassion. For example, when the leper implored Jesus for healing, saying, "If you will, you can make me clean." Mark records that Jesus "Moved with pity . . . stretched out his hand and touched him and said to him, 'I will; be clean'" (Mark 1:40-41). Again, before Jesus provided for the hungry crowd on one occasion, the Scripture records Jesus saying, "I have compassion on the crowd because they have been with me now three days and have nothing to eat" (Matt. 15:32).

The inspired apostle exhorts believers, "Put on . . . compassionate hearts" (Col. 3:12).

Kindness

Living in an age that by the day is increasingly becoming more and more uncivil, the Christian is to be a bright star of Christian kindness against a black backdrop of barbarities, impoliteness, and thankless incivilities.

If Jesus Christ was anything while walking upon this earth, he was kind. It wasn't a syrupy, mushy variety of kindness either. It was a kindness which was always consistent with his holiness.

How I have grieved on occasions when failing to manifest the kindness of Christ. And yes, I've had to return and ask for forgiveness. Some years ago, while sitting in my vehicle in a Wal-Mart parking lot, I saw an attendant pushing a train of shopping baskets right toward my pickup truck. I said to myself that from the looks of things, this lad would shortly bang into my truck. And he did just that. I got out of my truck and scolded him: "You should try to be more careful!" And he should have been — I think we all would agree. But I had no sooner said what I did than I knew I was wrong. It was not what I had said that was necessarily wrong, but the *way* I had said it. I was convicted by the Holy Spirit for not manifesting the kindness of Christ. The boy did better than I — he immediately apologized. I drove off feeling like a guilty *sinner*. I had momentarily dropped my guard. Becoming careless, I had allowed myself to think more of a twelve-year-old-year piece of steel and plastic than of how I might represent Christ to a stranger in a public parking lot.

By keeping our focus on the Man at God's right hand, we will be replenished with this Christian grace of kindness. God exhorts each of us, "Put on . . . kindness" (Col. 3:12).

Humility

To be humble is to know our place before God and before our fellows.

To paraphrase 1 Corinthians 13:

> Humility does not brag and it is not arrogant; it does not act unbecomingly and it is not selfish. It does not think more highly of itself than it should. It does not take credit where it shouldn't. And when it does experience some accomplishment, it sincerely gives God the glory and others the credit due them.

Humility is not self-absorbed. The truth is, it is self-forgetful. By focusing on ourselves, our needs and our rights, we become self-centered, proud people. By focusing on Jesus, who "humbled himself, by becoming obedient to the point of death, even the death on a cross" (Phil. 2:7), we will grow in humility and meekness. Humility's watchword and song is, "Christ must increase; I must decrease" (John 3:30).

Colossians 3:12 reads, "Put on . . . humility."

Gentleness

The same word is used in Galatians 6:1, where Paul exhorts mature believers to restore failing believers "in a spirit of gentleness." Earlier in the same epistle he informs us that gentleness is a product of the Spirit (5:23).

Sometimes it is easier to see the meaning of a word by seeing its opposite in action. The late New Testament Greek scholar, William Barclay (1907-1978), in commenting on the essence of the grace of gentleness shares an anecdote describing what it is not.

> Sir Joshua Reynolds said of Dr. Johnson: "The most light and airy dispute was with him a dispute in the arena. He fought on every occasion as if his whole reputation depended upon the victory of the minute, and he fought with all his weapons. If he was foiled in an argument, he had recourse to abuse and rudeness." After a vivid night at the Crown and Anchor, Johnson said contentedly to Boswell: "Well, we had a good talk." To which Boswell dutifully replied: "Yes, sir, you tossed and gored several persons." Goldsmith said of Johnson: "There is no arguing with Johnson for, when his pistol misses fire, he knocks you down with the butt end of it." Even the Rev. John Taylor who was a close friend of Johnson said of him: "There is no disputing with him. He will not hear you, and, having a louder voice than you must roar you down."[3]

Clearly, Samuel Johnson (1709-1784) and the grace of gentleness were strangers to each other. By keeping our eyes fastened on Jesus, we will become more and more gentle people. By our doing so, certainly the church and the world will be the beneficiaries.

Paul exhorts, "Put on . . . gentleness" (Col. 3:12 NASB).

Patience

The crucified, risen believer who is being transformed increasingly into the likeness of his Master, is to be characterized by the grace of patience. The context suggests that the word means the ability to act in forbearance toward others: "bearing with one another" (v. 13).

There is a difference between forbearance and forgiveness. When a brother or sister in Christ, for example, wrongs us, sins against us — the situation requires us to *forgive* the offending party. However, when we become annoyed, for example, by the behavior, or idiosyncrasies, or the bad manners, or crude conduct of a brother or sister in Christ, the grace of forgiveness is not required; instead, we are to *forbear,* or exercise the grace of *patience* toward this person.

Some people will naturally *rub us* the wrong way at times. And undoubtedly we do likewise. But if our spiritual gaze stays habitually focused on the Person at God's right hand, we will experience a renewed capacity to be patient toward all people. This can only happen as we walk day-by-day and moment-by-moment under the control of the Holy Spirit. Failing to do so, we become impulsive and impetuous; irritable, and short-tempered, even harsh.

God reminds us that since we have been raised up with Christ, we are to always be *seeking* things above; we are to have our minds *set* on things above. Where are those *things* located? They're found in the person of Jesus Christ, the Man at God's right hand. What are some of these things we are to be always seeking? They are: a compassionate heart, kindness, humility, gentleness, and patience.

Walking in the Spirit

Before finishing with this subject, it might be well to remind ourselves: there is no experience of grace promised to any Christian whereby God implants these graces into the heart at one stroke. It is only as the believer walks moment by moment, submitting to the lordship of Jesus Christ, with eyes fixed on him that the graces of the crucified, risen life will flourish in the hearts of God's people.

Nietzsche (1844-1900) once said of the Christians he knew, "You will have to look more redeemed, if I am to believe in your Redeemer." The world has a right to expect from Christians a resemblance to their Master. So do fellow Christians.

Thank God, through the blessed sanctifying ministries of the Holy Spirit, with our cooperation, he will shape us more and more into the likeness of the very image of Christ himself. This being the case, possibly there will be those who will eventually remark to their friends, "Beware, there goes a risen person!"

Love

The grace of love is the greatest of all graces. After exhorting believers to equip themselves with compassion, kindness, humility, gentleness, and patience, the apostle adds in Colossians 3:14, "And above all these put on love, which binds everything together in perfect harmony."

When the "love of God has been poured into our hearts through the Holy Spirit" (Rom. 5:5), and is being renewed day-by-day in the lives of God's people, Paul says this love "binds" all the graces — compassion, kindness, humility, gentleness, patience, and so much more — "together in perfect harmony."

Love — the very love of Christ — filling the hearts of Christ's people is the key to maintaining our fellowship with one another, and with the Lord Jesus Christ.

Charlotte Elliott's Prayer

Let this prayer of Charlotte Elliott's (1789-1871) express the deepest desire of our hearts:

Lord Jesus, make Thyself to me
A living, bright reality.
More present to faith's vision keen
Than any outward object seen,
More dear, more intimately nigh
Than e'en the sweetest earthly tie.[4]

CHAPTER 12

Wounded by God

S ome six hundred years before the Word became flesh, the prophet Isaiah was given a vision of God's Suffering Servant. Of this
One who was to bring healing, forgiveness, and reconciliation to Adam's fallen race, the ancient seer said, "Yet it was the LORD'S will to
crush him and cause him to suffer." (Isa. 53:10).[1] While reeling from
the unfriendly providences thrust upon him, righteous Job cries out
to God, "The arrows of the Almighty are in me" (Job 6:4).

There came a time when the patriarch Jacob was facing the chal-
lenge of his life. The very brother he had deceived twenty years previously is now approaching him with a band of men. As far as Jacob
knows, Esau has come to take his "pound of flesh." Jacob is desperate. He finds a place of solitude and the struggle begins . . . with
God . . . and within himself. God uses Jacob's critical circumstances to
show him *his* strength; he uses the occasion to open the eyes of Jacob
to his own inherent weaknesses and sinful proclivity.

Under pressure from the Almighty, broken Jacob readily
acknowledges that he was essentially a deceiver at heart, a manipula-
tor of people. God wounded him internally as well as externally in
order that he could bless him and use him more effectively. When
Jacob had fully surrendered to God's strength, thereafter he always
walked with a limp—a wound—a wound placed there by God so he
would never forget God's strength and his own vulnerability (see
Gen. 32:22-32).

The three previous examples are typical of God's dealings with those he wishes to use as instruments of his righteousness and grace.

We live in a religious age where we are constantly besieged by popular preachers and writers regarding God's willingness to heal — the "Name it and claim it prophets." I'm a strong believer in divine healing. I know what it is to be healed personally; and I have seen others through the years healed by the Lord in a definite way. I have always emphasized in my ministry God's willingness to heal the body according to his sovereign pleasure and purpose.

But in our search for healing, prosperity, success, and blessing from the Lord, we're sadly and tragically missing out on something immeasurably more important. While we're continually crying out to God to bless us, we have failed to realize that God may want to *wound* us, *bruise* us, *crush* us.

Jesus said that the servant is not above his Lord. Even the Father, in order to affect his sovereign plan of redemption, chose to "crush" his own Son, that he might bring eternal blessing to mankind: "it was the Lord's will to crush him. "

In our rush to be *successful* we have fought off being wounded by God; in our struggle to become *somebody* we have shied away from God's bruising blows to our self-centered egos and unsanctified ambitions. J. R. Miller (1840-1912) realized this and observed, "Whole, unbruised, unbroken men are of little use to God." A. W. Tozer (1897-1963) recognized the same truth when he said that those whom God chooses to bless greatly he must first wound deeply. There is no blessing apart from the blows. There is no resurrection without the cross.

An unknown writer has formed this truth in poetic verse:

When God wants to drill a man,
And thrill a man,
And skill a man
To play the noblest part;
When He yearns with all His heart
To create so great and bold a man
That all the world shall be amazed,
Watch His methods, watch His ways!

How He ruthlessly perfects
Whom He royally elects!
How He hammers him and hurts him,
And with mighty blows converts him
Into trial shapes of clay which
Only God understands;
While his tortured heart is crying
And he lifts beseeching hands!
How He bends but never breaks
When his good He undertakes;
How He uses whom He chooses,
And with every purpose fuses him:
By every act induces him
To try his splendor out —
God knows what He's about.[2]

When Jesus prayed in Gethsemane, "Not as I will, but as you will" (Matt. 26:39), he understood that he could not be the Father's instrument of atonement without surrendering to the Father's crushes. If Jesus as the Son of God could not accomplish his Father's will apart from accepting his Father's wounds, what makes us think we can accomplish the purposes of God apart from accepting his bruises?

Could it be that too many of our Lord's servants today are praying for God to bless them when, instead, the God and Father of our Lord Jesus Christ wants to wound them, bruise them, crush them? Too often our prayers consist of "Bless ME, bless ME, bless ME," when they should be "WOUND me, BRUISE me, CRUSH me."

God's wounds are necessary because of the tendency of our fallen nature to be proud. The Apostle Paul finally reached the point in his struggle over the "thorn" in his flesh where he understood God's purpose of the thorn. He wrote later that God sent it to "keep me from being too elated by the surpassing greatness of the revelations" (2 Cor. 12:7). How much pride is being flaunted in the body of Christ because God's servants have resisted the disciplining that comes from accepting God's piercing wounds in our points of pride.

When God chooses to wound his servants he selects the precise spots where they are the most vulnerable, the very places in their character and personality where a blow from God would cause them the most pain. He did this physically to Jacob by selecting one of man's most critical nerves — the sciatica. God struck his servant with a precision blow. He will do the same to us . . . if we don't run from the hand that would discipline us in love.

The God who wounded Jacob, Job, Paul, and his own Son, will wound his servants precisely where they need it the most. Why? In order to destroy us? Never! But because he is the Master Potter and wants to *make* us. Or, to change the metaphor, he takes our crushed egos, our wounded pride, our bitter failures, our defeated dreams — that he might create a divine fragrance, a heavenly aroma to ascend back to his throne. And when he smells the sweet smelling savor of his own making, he is pleased and rewarded. We want God to use our strengths; God wants to use our *wounds*. For God knows we are never stronger than when we are wounded. Because it is his wounds that make us weak in ourselves so that we might be strong in the Lord.

Once Martin Wells Knapp (1853-1901), the founding president of God's Bible School & College, was undergoing a painful trial. While in prayer one day, he asked the Lord to remove the problem. In relating this painful encounter, Lettie Cowman (1870-1960) wrote, "As he waited before the Lord the vision of a rough piece of marble rose before him with a sculptor grinding and chiseling. Watching the dust and chips fill the air, he noticed a beautiful image begin to appear in the marble."

Cowman proceeds to relate how the Lord spoke to Knapp and said, "Son, you are that block of marble. I have an image in mind, and desire to produce it in your character, and will do so if you will stand the grinding; but I will stop now if you so desire."

Knapp's resolute response was, "Lord, continue the chiseling and grinding."[3]

Years ago I copied on the flyleaf of one of my Bibles the following words which were written by Francis Asbury (1745-1816), American Methodism's premier pioneer circuit rider and leader: "Dear Lord, if Thou seest Thy servant will miss the way, in tender pity send a thorn deep into his side to drive him to Thy Christ and Thy Calvary."

I never realized the depth of those words as a young preacher.

However, I have since had the opportunity to experience the wounds of God: for it has been the Lord's will even to crush *me*. And I must say I have lived to kiss the *hands* which dealt the loving and measured blows.

It may take some time before we arrive at the place where we can joyfully thank the Lord for wounding us, for using *thorns* in the perfecting process. But if we hold lovingly and obediently steady — that day will come.

Free Church of Scotland pastor and hymn writer, George Matheson (1842-1906) — who is perhaps best known for his hymn "O Love That Will Not Let Me Go" — once confessed to his lack of gratitude for a most unpleasant providence (he became totally blind at age 20). While contemplating his unthankfulness one day, he wrote, "My God, I have never thanked Thee for my thorn! I have thanked Thee a thousand times for my roses, but never once for my thorn."

When it becomes the will of the Lord to crush us, to bruise us, to drive a thorn deep into our side, let us so abide in Christ until what is lacking is us is perfected by the loving wounds of mercy: "After you have suffered for a little while, the God of all grace, who called you to His eternal glory in Christ, will Himself perfect, confirm, strengthen *and* establish you. To Him *be* dominion forever and ever. Amen" (1 Pet. 5:10-11 NASB).

Though You have crushed me, O Lord,
I have lived to see Your wisdom and goodness.
I bless Your name for the wounds,
Kissing the hands molding me into wholeness.

CHAPTER 13

From Gold to God

On a beautiful fall afternoon in October 2001, my wife and I interviewed the subject of this article, Sir Durward Knowles. Sitting in his spacious living room overlooking a placid Nassau Bay, we were anxious to hear this octogenarian seaman share how his spiritual voyage finally brought him to faith in Christ two years prior to this occasion. Emily and I will always cherish the six days Sir Durward and Lady Holly entertained us in their lovely home. It was my privilege to conduct meetings on two separate occasions in their home church, Ebenezer Methodist Church in Nassau.

It was a lovely spring day in the Bahamas as Sir Durward Knowles walked into the lobby of the Nassau Radisson Hotel in May of 2000.

Durward was attending a seminar sponsored by his own Methodist Church Conference. As he read the schedule of the various seminar offerings, one caught his attention: "True Church Membership," which was to be jointly led by his pastor, Milton Lightbourne, and fellow Ebenezer Methodist Church member, Sidney Pender. Because of his high regard for these two presenters, Durward made his way to the designated room, took his seat beside Lady Holly, his lovely and devoted wife of 53 years, then sat back to listen.

As Durward listened intently to both speakers explain what true church membership was all about, and how one could be a church member without necessarily being a true Christian, Durward's conscience became strongly convicted by the Holy Spirit. He was in trouble.

Here he was, an 82-year-old lifelong church member, trustee, and respected civic leader, but he knew in his heart of hearts that he was not right with God. What should he do about it—if anything? A battle was raging.

Born to Sail

Water courses through Durward's veins. He was born in a house built by his father, located across the street from beautiful Nassau Harbor. Raised on a relatively small island—New Providence—he grew up in a culture where sailing came quite naturally. As a child, he would often go to the third floor of their house and gaze upon the waters, dreaming that one day he too would pilot ships, just as his father, Captain Harry Knowles did as a harbor pilot, in charge of taking ships in and out of Nassau.

Learning the ways of the sea from his well-respected father, this poor island boy upon graduating from Queens College, Nassau, embarked upon a journey that would eventually take him from Nassau Harbor, to an Olympic gold medal, to a harbor pilot captain, to being knighted by the Queen of England, to a living faith in Jesus Christ.

For as far back as he can remember, Durward always wanted to ply the seas. As a youngster, his father implanted such a desire in his son as he often regaled the family with seafaring stories as well as relating his own colorful experiences as a harbor pilot. Young Durward began to anticipate the day that he, too, would be called "Captain Knowles," just like his father. As Providence would have it, he became more than a captain.

His sailing career began on Nassau Harbor and Montagu Bay in a small craft called a "smack." From those humble sailing origins, he eventually gained a reputation for being one of Nassau's best young sailors. He loved the sea; he loved sailing; he loved competition. But life was not all fun. Though Durward enjoyed racing off Nassau's shores, he knew also that he must earn a living for himself. Thus, he set out to become a harbor pilot. But after serving as an apprentice for five years, there were no openings in this exclusive enterprise. Therefore, he opted to hire on with a freight shipping company, where eventually he would become the captain of his own ship.

The Quest for Gold

When he was not occupied with earning a living, Durward could be found sailing on Montagu Bay, commanding a Star class racing yacht. Eventually he developed into one of the best Star boat skippers at the Nassau Yacht Club.

Having gained sufficient confidence in his racing skills, by the time 1946 arrived, this fledgling racer made the decision to enter the Star World Championships to be held in Cuba. Believing that he needed a better yacht in order to be competitive, he took his life savings and purchased a boat named *Gem*, which would be the first of many Star boats he owned by that name—a name that he would make famous in nautical history.

Despite inferior sails, Durward placed third in the Cuba competition, which was a great surprise to competitors far more experienced than he. From Cuba, this young island boy's racing career and sailing reputation began to expand until he was entering every race he possibly could. In 1947 he entered the Los Angeles World Championships in the Star class, and took first place with his crew. It was an exhilarating experience.

After Los Angeles, Durward made the decision to go for the gold—to enter his first Olympic competition. The 1948 summer Olympics were to be held in England. Proudly representing his native land, this Bahamian lad of European stock, set out with his crew to make his countrymen proud.

But 1948 was not to be his year. Although well positioned to win the gold medal, tragedy struck in the final race—the mast cracked, and with it their hopes. "I don't think I've ever been more disappointed in my sailing career than when that mast went overboard," Knowles recalled.[1]

Although he competed in the 1952 Helsinki Games, no medals were won. It was the 1956 Melbourne Games where Captain Knowles and his crew captured a bronze medal—the first ever for any Bahamian. He and his crew arrived back in Nassau to a joyous large crowd at the airport. It was an unforgettable Olympics as well as a memorable celebration with his beloved islanders.

Between the Olympic Games he raced in a variety of competitive events, but Durward wouldn't be satisfied until he won the ultimate for his country — Olympic gold! "We realized that we had won everything else in the Star class and the only thing left was the Olympic gold. Italy seemed to be the year for us. After winning the Pan American Games, we felt we had an excellent chance," he related.[2] However, the 1960 Games in Naples turned out to be a bitter disappointment. Not only was no gold won — he and his crew never placed.

But one virtue Durward has never lacked is perseverance. Following the disappointing 1960 Games, he sold his boat and ordered another to be built by an excellent craftsman, who was himself an expert in the Star class. With a new yacht in hand, he and his crew won the gold in the 1962 Commonwealth Games in Jamaica.

However, Olympic gold was what he wanted. Thus, careful plans were made and all necessary details attended to before his arrival in Tokyo for the 1964 Olympic Games. He was confident upon arriving in Japan that he possessed a worthy vessel, a capable crew, and experienced skills to bring honor worthy of his country.

Before the seventh and final race of the Star class event, he received the following telegram from the Duke of Edinburgh, Prince Philip, whom he had taken for a sail once on Montagu Bay: "Visiting Nassau and remember our splendid sail. We are praying you will gain a gold medal for the Bahamas."[3]

As would any aspiring Olympic competitor, Durward went to bed that night dreaming of what the next day might bring. Could it be that he would finally achieve his dream of dreams? Or was it going to be only a dream?

His dream came true. Coming from seventh place in the race's final leg, he and his crew coached Gem to first place and the long-coveted gold medal. Three decades later Durward recalled: "There is no way I can describe my emotions at that moment. There is nothing to compare to that point in my life. It was a thrill beyond all thrills, a high beyond all highs. It was the culmination of my ultimate dreams. I had done it! I had won a gold medal in the Olympic Games!"

Before his Olympic days were finished, Durward would compete in a total of eight Games. His last was to be in Seoul, South Korea in 1988 at age 70! While he was disinclined to race in Seoul because of his age, at the urging of his many friends he decided to compete in the Games for the last time.

In an interview before leaving Nassau, Durward said, "I'm only going for the Bahamas. The truth is, I know I'm not going to win a medal. But I'm going to be carrying the flag for the Bahamas and I'm hoping NBC will focus its camera on this old fella' carrying his country's flag and they'll find something good to say about us."[4] Only two men have been older Olympians.

As predicted, a medal wasn't in the picture for Durward in his final Olympic Games. However, the exposure he brought to his country as a seven-decades-old-competitor was almost as gratifying as winning a gold medal. His Olympic days were over; he had represented his country admirably for forty years.

A Harbor Pilot

Running parallel with his early dream to bring Olympic gold back to his homeland was Durward's aspiration to be a Nassau harbor pilot, just like his father. Because of his arthritic problems, Captain Harry Knowles retired in 1953 from piloting ships in and out of Nassau Bay, thus recreating an opening for his son.

In this island community, a harbor pilot is one of the most respected positions. Nassau, being one of the prominent stops for international cruise lines, as well as an active harbor for freighters, harbor pilots are kept busy expertly guiding these ships around shoals unknown to the visiting ship's captains.

Durward is celebrating his fiftieth anniversary this year (2002) as a harbor pilot. Still rising in the early morning hours, this sea-worn sailor drives to Nassau Bay, climbs into a little boat which ferries him alongside a cruise ship, climbs up a long ladder to the liner's deck, makes his way to the helm, thereupon coaching the pilot as he enters — or leaves — Nassau Harbor.

He never feels more at home than when he's at a ship's helm. He was born to sail.

Knighted by the Queen

With the recognition, which came to Durward as a result of his outstanding sailing accomplishments, as well as his several prosperous financial investments, he has become one of the Bahamas' foremost civic leaders and philanthropists.

Serving as the founder, director, vice president and chairman of a multiplicity of civic societies and not-for-profit organizations, this gentle, kind, and wise man has made a lasting mark upon his city, country, and friends.

Many people have benefited through the years because of Durward's benevolent generosity. Whether it has been his local church or conference in need of a substantial donation beyond his regular giving, or impoverished strangers knocking on his office door seeking funds to pay their rent, or the donation of hundreds of wheelchairs for the handicapped, or paying the medical bills for a needy acquaintance—this man has given back to his church and community in ways that most will never know, and I might add, he is very reluctant to share.

Durward's gracious humanitarian involvement through the years eventually moved Prime Minister Ingraham in 1996, to recommend to Her Majesty, Queen Elizabeth, that Durward be knighted.

When that momentous day finally arrived for his entry into one of history's most celebrated societies, Durward recalls, "Just entering Buckingham Palace was enough for me." But he was there for something more than to gaze upon royal ornate architecture.

Upon being ushered into the presence of the Queen, he fondly remembers, "I was bowing to the Queen, moving forward, bowing again, touched on my right shoulder, then on the left by the Queen's royal sword. The Queen spoke, we shook hands, and I was a knight!" Thereafter it would be "Sir Durward" and "Lady Holly." Durward is only the second nonpolitical person in Bahamian history with this esteemed title.

Something More

Though he had been baptized and confirmed as a child in his local church, and was regular in his Sunday morning worship, Holly had been praying for years that Durward would come to an authentic faith in Christ.

What had prevented this well-respected churchman and notable community leader from making a total surrender to the Lord Jesus

Christ?

In moving somber tones, with tears forming in his piercing sea-blue eyes, Durward reflected, "I thought I was a good person, helping people. In my position in the community and everything, I had a lot of pride. All my accomplishments and stature in the community created that feeling of pride." "But," he continued, whenever I listened to good preaching, I knew something was missing; I was made conscious that I needed something more than what I had."

As it turned out, that "something more" was "Someone" more. After all his sailing achievements and civic recognitions; after winning the Olympic gold, and being knighted by the Queen of England; after being applauded by the millions, as well as accumulating a substantial financial portfolio—he was empty and hungry inside.

The Narrow Gate

All who come to faith in Jesus Christ walk through the same gate—the narrow gate. It is narrow because in walking through this gate, we renounce all self-righteousness and trust in our own good works, casting ourselves down before a merciful God who has provided an atonement for all repentant sinners through his Son, the Lord Jesus Christ. This was the gate Durward faced as he sat in the conference room listening to his pastor and lay leader explain what it meant to be a real Christian.

At the close of the seminar, Durward knew what he must do. Moved by the poignant conviction of the Spirit of God, he humbled himself, walked to the front of the room and asked to speak with Pastor Lightbourne and Sidney Pender.

"Men," he confessed in total honesty, "I know in my heart that I am not right with God; I don't think I have ever trusted fully in Jesus Christ. Would you pray for me?"

Standing shoulder to shoulder in a tight circle, prayer was made to God for the salvation of this Nassau seaman and Methodist Church member. And his prayer was heard. For the first time in his life, Durward says, "I experienced a peace and confidence in my heart."

Changes

Prior to this event, Durward had only attended the services of his church on Sunday mornings. That immediately changed. The following Wednesday evening he was in prayer meeting (some Methodist churches still have them!). And for the first time, he stood to his feet and spontaneously gave an authentic confession of faith in Jesus Christ as his Lord and Savior. Two months later while at a family gathering hosted by his brother, once again Durward testified to his faith in Christ. He still faithfully attends prayer meeting and Sunday evening services, in addition to Sunday morning worship. And I might add, he was in all the meetings I conducted the two times I was a guest preacher at Ebenezer Methodist Church.

Durward transparently acknowledges, however, "I don't feel comfortable about praying in public." And then adding with a bit of English wit, "But I must admit, if I could, I wouldn't pray as long as some people do!"

Some humorous rejoinder is never far from the tip of Durward's tongue. For example, Lady Holly graciously provided me with a pitcher of water each night during a recent seminar I conducted in their church. Durward told me after each service, "I sure hoped that you wouldn't drink any water tonight; I was afraid it would encourage you to speak longer!" Then he would break out into one of his broadest smiles. I think I detected a bit of Heaven's light beaming from that broad countenance.

The story of Durward Knowles' remarkable spiritual voyage affirms our faith in a merciful, persevering God. It also points out the sad reality that many people in our churches, who although they are members, do not have a saving faith in the Lord Jesus Christ. May the odyssey of this brother in Christ encourage each of us to make our calling and election sure.

There is mercy higher than the heavens;
There is grace deeper than the seas.
There is pardon for the sinner —
For each who in Christ sincerely believes.

CHAPTER 14

When God Comes Near
(Part 1)

The Bible teaches us that God is everywhere present in his creation. The psalmist affirmed this truth when he prayed, "You know when I sit down and when I rise up; you discern my thoughts from afar. You search out my path and my lying down and are acquainted with all my ways" (Psa. 139:2-3).[1] Expanding further on this subject, he inquired of the Lord in verses 7-8, "Where shall I go from your Spirit? Or where shall I flee from your presence? If I ascend to heaven, you are there! If I make my bed in Sheol, you are there." Theologians refer to this everywhere-present attribute of God as omnipresence.

But there is another dimension to the presence of God that requires our attention. Those who are students of the Word of God, as well as experienced in the ways of God, know that God comes near and is present in the lives of God-seekers in a way he is not near and present among the rest of humankind. Some refer to this activity as the *manifest presence of God*: God communicating with ordinary Christians like you and me — people who are characteristically hungry and thirsty for God.

Something with the mark of the Eternal stamped upon it inevitably occurs when God and the God-seeker encounter one another. What impact that encounter has on us will vary depending upon what one's need is at the time. But we can rest assured of this: Before that Divine rendezvous is over, we will know in our spirit that we have been in the presence of God like Jacob of old when he exclaimed, "How awesome is this place" (Gen. 28:17)!

What actually happens when God comes near to us by his Holy Spirit?

Conviction of Sin

Webster's dictionary won't help us understand what conviction of sin is all about, but all who have experienced the persuasive influence of the Holy Spirit indicting one's own conscience of unacceptable behavior (sin) — these know what conviction of sin is.

Jesus said of the Holy Spirit, "And when he comes, he will convict the world concerning sin . . ." (John 16:8). It is impossible for a sinner to trust Christ as Lord and Savior without this prerequisite conviction of sin.

"I've been reading a friend of yours," said a young man to theologian J.I. Packer leaving church one Sunday morning. "I think he knows me."

"Who is it?" asked Packer.

"John Owen. He seems to know exactly what's going on inside me . . ."[2]

It's true, John Owen (1616-1683) embodied the best of Puritan devotion: the awe of God, humility, wisdom, and an awareness of God's grace. He also dealt with the nature of sinful humanity as few writers have done as keenly or thoroughly. But it is the Holy Spirit who really knows what's going on inside of us, not John Owen (though God uses human instruments in Spirit-conviction): "And no creature is hidden from his sight, but all are naked and exposed to the eyes of him to whom we must give account" (Heb. 4:13).

As a sixteen-year-old boy kneeling at an altar of prayer, it was the Holy Spirit who uncovered layers of transgressions in my sinful, broken heart. He reminded me of the grapes I had stolen from a produce counter in the local A & P grocery store; of Cokes I had taken unlawfully from a soda machine; of the many unkindnesses I had committed against my step-mother; and of the moral impurities of a wicked heart. But fundamentally he showed me that I had sinned against him, a holy God.[3]

Sin is an offense against the character and person of God; it's a violation of his holy law, a transgression of his revealed will. Sin is an enemy of God. Sin is a failure to perfectly obey the revealed will of God; it's a failure to love as Christ loved. However, sin should not only be thought of as an unholy act, but also as a moral pollution, an unholy disease, the bent of the will toward evil.

The only way one can be brought face to face with his or her own sin is through the personal, pungent, convicting ministries of the blessed Holy Spirit. The Spirit uses many and varied means to this end: the spoken Word of God, the creation of God (Martin Luther was reminded of his barren, sinful life upon seeing a leafless tree one winter); the Christlike life of a devout believer; providential happenings (such as a death, divorce, or illness); inner emptiness and a sense of aloneness. Through any one of these, as well as many other providential circumstances, the Spirit of God draws people to the Lord Jesus Christ.

Here is where the church and her ministering servants play such a vital and necessary role in Kingdom work. God's primary means of reaching people — and conviction of sin is a necessary means to that end — is his written and spoken Word.

God uses his Word in at least three different forms: the *read* Word of God; the *spoken* Word of God, and the *lived* Word of God (incarnational Word). We'll concern ourselves here with two of these.

Conviction of Sin and the Read Word of God

The Holy Spirit again and again uses the read Word of God to bring conviction to the hearts of the reader. Whether it is a traveling businessman reaching into a desk drawer for a Gideon's Bible before he retires for the night, and upon reading is convicted of his sins, or a gospel tract providentially falling into the hands of some desperate God-seeker, or in the privacy of one's own home with an open Bible on the lap, the Word of God is God's primary agent in arresting guilty sinners. "For the word of God is living and active, sharper than any two-edged sword, piercing to the division of soul and of spirit, of joints and of marrow, and discerning the thoughts and intentions of the heart" (Heb. 4:12).

Thus the importance of Christians engaging in both Bible distribution and Bible reading. Thank God for every ministry engaged in

Bible distribution—ministries like Voice of the Martyrs, for example, which in 1994 floated 80,000 Scripture balloons into closed North Korea. Or, like a team from our church who recently distributed 7,000 Bibles in China.

Conviction of Sin and the Spoken Word of God

All God's people have a responsibility and privilege to speak his Word as opportunities arise. As those who believe in the priesthood of all believers, we evangelicals don't—or, shouldn't—leave to vocational clergy the sole responsibility of sharing the Word of God. The spoken Word of God can have a powerful effect upon the hearer, whether it's spoken by a so-called layperson or one employed in full-time vocational ministry.

Even so, preachers do have a unique responsibility. It is their special calling to preach and teach the whole counsel of God, and to proclaim the everlasting gospel of Jesus Christ. They are called by God to do this, not in their own strength, but through the enabling power of the Holy Spirit. "'Not by might, nor by power, but by my Spirit,' says the Lord of hosts" (Zech. 4:6). Paul reminded the Thessalonian believers, "our gospel came to you not only in word, but also in power and in the Holy Spirit and with full conviction" (1 Thess. 1:6). What an awesome calling!

Wherever and whenever this Word is spoken, if it is to have its maximum effect, it must be spoken by a person God can use. When God seeks to reach the unsaved, he sends a prepared person across their path with the gospel message; when he seeks to revive and restore his wandering sheep, he raises up a God-anointed individual to reach them. Whether this spoken Word is shared in a corporate setting (e.g., a Sunday worship service), or one-on-one with an individual (e.g., Philip with the Ethiopian), apart from the convicting presence of the Holy Spirit, the work of God will not be effective.

God's plan to reach needy people is not merely Bible distribution, or else he wouldn't need preachers. God's normal plan in reaching men and women with the gospel of Jesus Christ is to call, cleanse, equip, and fill his ministering servants with the Holy Spirit. It's the Holy Spirit working through a God-filled person when the Word of God is spoken that has great power. And whenever this is accompanied by a contingent of God-filled, praying saints in the pews, sinners will be convicted of their sins and careless Christians will be convicted of theirs as well.

If I could, I would shout this truth from the pulpit of every church in America: "It's the Holy Spirit! It's the Holy Spirit! It's the Holy Spirit!" Without him all our Bible studies, sermons, seminars, prayers, songs, lovely sanctuaries, degrees, choirs and orchestras are absolutely worthless — worthless. One of the greatest needs in our churches is Holy Spirit conviction!

Has the church forgotten how to do God's work in God's way? Listen to the late Times Square Church pastor David Wilkerson's (1931-2011) assessment of our dilemma:

> We constantly hear awful exaggerations about the numbers of people who come to Jesus through various ministries. Christians report scores of people were saved as they preached in prisons, schools, tribal meetings. They say, "Everybody in the place gave his heart to Jesus. When I finished preaching, they came forward for salvation."
>
> No — that is a tragic exaggeration! All too often, what actually happens is that everyone simply repeats a prayer. They merely pray what they're told to pray — and few of them grasp what they're saying. Then most of them go back to their heathen ways!

Then Wilkerson reasons:

> I believe the church has even taken the feeling out of conviction. Think about it—you hardly ever see tears on the cheeks of those who are being *saved* anymore. Of course, I know tears don't save anyone. But God made us all human, with very real feelings. And any hell-bound sinner who has been moved by the Holy Spirit naturally feels a profound sorrow over the ways he has grieved the Lord.[4]

Alcibiades once said to Socrates: "Socrates, I hate you; for every time I see you, you show me what I am." And so it is with God; he strips us of all the veneer, makeup and pretense. He tears away our facade and cover-up, and then shows us what we are and who we are—if we listen, if we bow down low enough, if we stay long enough.

Joseph is a Stranger

The children of Israel's troubles began when "there arose a new king over Egypt, who did not know Joseph" (Ex. 1:8). The churches' troubles begin whenever we have pastors, church leaders and members who are brought into the church without ever being convicted of their sins, without ever being truly changed. The language of Spirit-conviction is totally foreign to them—they do not know *Joseph,* as it were. They are unfamiliar with godliness, righteousness, holiness and divine truth. They introduce into the church the ways of Egypt, the ways of the world. They say it is better than before. Jesus walks away weeping.

I realize the picture I've just painted is not the condition of every church, and it may not be the condition of yours. But who among us can be satisfied? If it's not the condition of your church, shouldn't we be burdened for neighboring churches and the Church at-large? What can we do that we might experience a greater degree of the *manifest* presence of God among us?

Pray

Pray for yourself. Ask yourself before God: Am I a truly converted person? Have I been born again? Am I living a fully surrendered and obedient life? Is there sin in my life? Make sure you are thoroughly right with God and then, by his grace, walk in the light of God, keeping in step with the Spirit of God.

Secondly, pray for your church. Pray for its leaders. Pray for its services. Pray that God will be pleased to send a fresh visitation of the Holy Spirit your way. Don't be critical of your leaders and fellow members. Oswald Chambers once wrote: "God gives his people the Spirit of discernment for the purpose of intercession, not for the purpose of criticism." Pray, pray, pray. Love, love, love. Believe, believe, believe!

What actually happens when God comes near in his *manifest*

presence? One of the undeniable marks of the presence of God is conviction of sin—Holy Spirit conviction. Where the Spirit is welcome
and present, sinners will be convicted of their *sins* and Christians will
be convicted of their failure to be more Christlike.

Our singing, prayers, and preaching
Are shallow and vacuous sounds,
Until the Lord himself appears,
Revealing His five bleeding wounds.

Our motions at worship and Word
Leave us empty on the inside,
Unless our hearts are touched by God,
And He alone is glorified.

CHAPTER 15

When God Comes Near
(Part 2)

As mentioned in the previous chapter, God is not only omnipresent in his creation, he is also present in a special way among those whom we might call God-seekers and Christ-followers.

We saw that one of the spiritual principles of the kingdom of God is that whenever God comes near—i.e., manifests himself through his Holy Spirit to a God-seeker—one of the results will be conviction of sin in the life of the sinner as well as in the life of a failing Christian. The outshining of God's perfect holiness awakens in both the sinner and the Christian the awareness that all is not well whenever sin is near.

When God came near to a disobedient king, he lamented, "For I know my transgressions, and my sin is always before me" (Psa. 51:3).[1] When God came near to an unclean prophet, with deep agony of soul he cried out, "Woe is me! For I am lost . . . for my eyes have seen the King, the LORD of hosts!" (Isa. 6:5). When God came near to an unbelieving disciple, he instinctively cried out, "Depart from me, for I am a sinful man, O Lord!" (Luke 5:8). Holy Spirit conviction of sin invariably accompanies the manifest presence of God when sin is present.

The purpose of God in convicting the conscience of sin is that he might bring us into fellowship with himself and conform us to the likeness of his Son, the Lord Jesus Christ" (see Rom. 8:29). If we confess whatever God convicts us of, there is mercy and restoration (see

1 John 1:7).

Hungering for Holiness

But there is more. Not only does God convict of sin whenever he manifests himself to sinners and failing Christians, he also creates in them a hunger for holiness — the holiness we see manifested in our Exemplar, the Lord Jesus Christ.

Any so-called decision for Christ that is unaccompanied by a hunger for holiness, is a spurious conversion. Any baptismal candidate who has failed to discover an intense appetite for holiness of heart and life following a walk down the sanctuary aisle, will come out of the baptismal waters as much a sinner as when he or she descended into the waters.

The same convicted king who lamented, "For I know my transgressions, and my sin is always before me" — also prayed, "Create in me a clean heart, O God, and renew a right spirit within me" (Psa. 51:10). The same convicted prophet who prayed, "Woe is me! For I am lost . . . for my eyes have seen the King, the LORD of hosts!" — also wrote, "And a highway shall be there, and it shall be called the Way of Holiness. The unclean shall not pass over it. It shall belong to those who walk on the way" (Isa. 35:8). The same convicted disciple who cried out, "Depart from me, for I am a sinful man, O Lord!" — also exhorted, "but as he who called you is holy, you also be holy in all your conduct; since it is written: 'You shall be holy, for I am holy,'" (1 Pet. 1:15-16).

One of the great tragedies of our day is that we are filling our church membership roles with people who do not evidence an intense appetite for God. Their lives are still characterized by the lusts of the flesh, the lusts of the eyes, and the pride of life (see 1 John 2:15-16). They're still in love with the world; they never left it! They still look like it, talk like it, smell like it, think like it, and walk like it.

A Soft Gospel

Is this a hard gospel? May I be so bold as to say that if this sounds to our dull, "uncircumcised" ears like a hard gospel, it is because we have grown accustomed to listening to a soft gospel, which is no gospel at all?

A soft gospel teaches Romans 7 without explaining Romans 8. A soft gospel tells people, "Neither do I condemn you," but doesn't say, "Go your way and sin no more" (see John 8:11). A soft gospel tells converts that they are clothed with the righteousness of Christ, but God doesn't expect them to keep their robes white. A soft gospel emphasizes the doctrine of justification, but has little, if anything, to say about the doctrine of sanctification. A soft gospel tells people to love God and others but has nothing to say about hating and forsaking sin.

A Change of Appetites

The Holy Spirit is called the *Holy* Spirit, not only because he himself is perfectly holy, but also because his primary mission is to conform believers to the likeness of Jesus Christ, which is Christian holiness.

When God comes near to a convicted, confessing sinner, who responds to God's gracious overtures with a simple evangelical faith in Christ, he imparts to such his Holy Spirit (see Rom. 8:10, 15). The Holy Spirit then begins his mission—not merely to get this believer to Heaven eventually—but to make this believer into the image of Christ.

A genuinely repentant believer soon discerns a change of spiritual and moral appetites. He probably won't be able to explain it theologically at the time, or even be able to quote a chapter and verse in the Bible to explain this evolving change. But he will intuitively know that a radical change is in the making. Although experiences will vary from person to person, a changed moral appetite is the universal, common denominator in every conversion.

An Example

After 50 years in India as a Methodist missionary, and after more than sixty years following his conversion to Christ, Dr. E. Stanley Jones wrote about the immediate change the Holy Spirit produced in him when he gave his heart and life to Jesus Christ:

> When I walked out the next morning following my conversion, I walked out into a new world. The trees seemed to clap

their hands; the sky was never so blue, and nature was never so alive and radiant. I walked up to my chum, Ras, slapped him on the back, and said, "My, what a d— fine day," using the old vocabulary to express my newfound joy. The angels must have smiled and said, "He's trying to say 'Hallelujah,' but he doesn't know the language yet. Let him alone; he'll get it." I said to myself: "Why, I can't say that again. I'm convert-ed." And it dropped away. I was to find a new vocabulary for a new type of life, for he converts us and our vocabulary. . . .

Sometimes while going to church the gang on the street corner would call out: "Hello, Stan, going down to see Je-sus?" And the inward answer was "Yes, glory be!" For going to church is just like that—"to see Jesus." But their taunts grew fainter and fainter and finally died as they saw I was lost to their crowd. I was marching to the beat of another Drummer, and I was trying to keep step with him . . .

One area of adjustment was made the next day after my conversion. Out of habit I went to the barber shop where a group used to play cards. But fortunately and providentially I picked up a pocket New Testament lying on a table in our home and took it with me. And it was lucky that I did, for it helped me break a useless and harmful tie. As the group gathered at the card table, I went to the barber's chair and began to read the New Testament. They called me to join them as usual in the card game. I replied: "No, I've been con-verted." It was a bomb. A silence fell upon the stunned group. One of them, Ras, who had refused to take the step when I took it [the day before], spoke up and said: "Well, then, read us something from that book."[2]

Amazing, isn't it?—the Holy Spirit jealousy beginning the pro-cess of forming the new-born believer into the likeness of the Lord Jesus Christ!

For every true conversion to Christ there are the attendant conse-quences—one of which is a hunger for holiness, which results in an immediate as well as ongoing change of life and lifestyle. (A note of caution: though such a radical change will not be seen in a young child, the fruit of conversion will be the same.)

Cultivating an Appetite for God

We can't give ourselves an appetite for God and holiness any more than a rock can call up an appetite for water. Apart from grace, we are dead to God; without the life of God in us, there can be no appetite for God. But although we cannot create within ourselves a hunger for God, we can take measures to cultivate and encourage the appetite he first gave us when we trusted in Christ. How can we cultivate and maintain a healthy appetite for God?

Consider the following pointers.

Give yourself to God totally. One cannot maintain a strong, healthy appetite for God and be a straddler. God wants you to serve him without reservation, with a single-mindedness of intention and will. To do this you must make a decisive, deliberate surrender of yourself to God. To those debating about taking such a step, the Apostle James exhorts: "purify your hearts, you double-minded." To those who have yet to make a complete consecration of themselves to God, the Holy Spirit pleads: "I appeal to you therefore, brothers, by the mercies of God, to present your bodies as a living sacrifice, holy and acceptable to God, which is your spiritual worship. Do not be conformed to this world, but be transformed by the renewal of your mind, that by testing you may discern what is the will of God, what is good and acceptable and perfect" (Rom. 12:1-2). Such a consecration will be affirmed again and again in the life of the hungry-hearted believer.

Meet with God regularly. I remember Mary Ann saying to me in a discipleship class soon after she gave her heart to Christ a number of years ago: "Pastor Tilley, I've cleaned out a spare bedroom where I can have my daily devotions." No one told her to do this. She did it because she wanted to have a quiet place where she could regularly meet with her new-found Friend.

A Christian without a systematic, regular devotional life is an undisciplined, careless Christian. To hunger after God is to set aside time to meet with him in his Word and to talk with him (prayer). Private Bible reading and prayer is a matter of spending time with our Friend.

Walk in the light explicitly. Your fallen sinful nature (the flesh) will provide you with a thousand reasons as to why you shouldn't obey the plain, revealed, written Word of God. But as a Christian, you are called to walk in the Spirit, not to walk after the flesh (see Gal. 5). By walking in the light (truth the Holy Spirit reveals to you through his Word directly, or by other means which are in harmony with his Word) you will enjoy uninterrupted fellowship with God, and maintain a healthy spiritual appetite.

Pray to God transparently. A. W. Tozer (1897-1963) once wrote that the only prayers that God responds to are *honest* prayers. There is so much phoniness in much of our praying because we ourselves are living a phony life.

When God comes near to us in our personal devotions, it's not a time for us to boast before God—we have nothing to boast of. It's a time of humbling oneself before God. It's a time for confessing: our lack of passion for God, our careless words, our deadness of spirit, our dry eyes, and our lack of zeal in reaching out to the lost.

Let's quit pretending before God. The last time I looked, a synonym for pretense was "hypocrite." God rewards transparent prayers and transparent people with his presence and blessings. Transparency before God engenders a greater appetite for God.

Abide in Christ Constantly. To learn to abide in Christ is one of the open secrets to a life of power and fruitfulness in the Christian life. To abide in Christ is to exchange our inability for his ability, to exchange our self-sufficiency for his all-sufficiency, to exchange our independence for his power and control. "Abide in me," Jesus says to every thirsty-hearted disciple (see John 15).

Are you enjoying God's nearness in your life? Are you experiencing a real, ongoing hunger for God—a hunger for his holiness? Jesus promised, "Blessed are those who hunger and thirst for righteousness, for they shall be satisfied" (Matt. 5:6). And they will be filled and satisfied again and again, and again—as long as they are hungry.

In closing I encourage you to join with me—an unworthy servant of the Lord Jesus—in affirming the ancient psalmist's confession:

"But for me it is good to be near God" (Psa. 73:28). Secondly, I ask you to join with me in supplicating our Father in Heaven:

O God, my Father, I thank you for coming near to us by sending your Son, the Lord Jesus Christ, into this fallen world. I thank you for coming near to me, by sending your Holy Spirit to inhabit my body – your sacred temple of clay. I cherish your nearness. Guard me, so I will not grieve your Holy Spirit and thereby lose your nearness. But when I do become careless, I beg of you to convict me of my failure, so your loving intimacy and nearness will return. Amen.

CHAPTER 16

A Praying Prophet

P rophets were—and are—uniquely gifted by God.
For one thing, prophets were seers. They were originally called such because they had insight and discernment unlike others. God had revealed to these men—and occasionally women—in sovereignly selected moments, the condition of nations, churches and individuals, as well as the foretelling of events.

No man chose to be a prophet. They were called and commissioned by God alone. Kings and priests under the Old Covenant, and pastors and evangelists under the New Covenant, were called by God and set apart for ministry by constituted authority. Not so with the prophets. They were accountable to God alone. They could neither be hired nor fired. No man or organization employed them. They were on no institution's payroll; they stood for no election; they were God's special agents.

The life of a prophet could be lonely because the masses and religious hierarchy often misunderstood his ministry. Because his messages were personally convicting, they were mostly dreaded and avoided. After all, who enjoys hearing, "Thou art the man!" or being called a "generation of vipers"? These men weren't given "Preacher of the Year" awards or standing ovations at the annual church conferences. They were a different breed.

Because of the nature of the prophet's role, it was vitally important that he walk close with God—that he be a person of prayer.

For without a praying heart the prophet would have become censorious and judgmental, even melancholy. With a praying heart he could deliver his messages faithfully and lovingly, and walk before God in joy and gratitude. Samuel was this kind of prophet—he was a praying prophet.

A Product of Prayer

Samuel was a product of prayer, for following his birth his mother exclaimed: "For this boy I prayed, and the LORD has given me my petition which I asked of him" (1 Sam. 1:27).[1] Just as there would have been no Augustine without a praying Monica, surely there would have been no Samuel without a praying Hannah.

As it is in the natural world, with plants and animals producing after their kind, so it often is in the spiritual world—praying parents beget praying children. At least this was true in the case of Samuel. He learned to pray early. No doubt he heard his parents, Elkanah and Hannah, pray often. And just as surely, he heard his mentor and priest, Eli, offer repeated heart-felt cries and petitions to Yahweh.

The sanctuary atmosphere in which he grew up was punctuated regularly with petitioners offering their confessions, thanksgivings and intercessions before God. When hearing the deep-felt prayers of godly, earnest worshipers forever shaped the appetite of this young prophet-in-waiting—for prayer was the very language of sanctuary worship.

A Reputation for Prayer

Having learned to discern the voice of God at a young age,[2] Samuel went on to become one of Israel's foremost prophets. The one thing which characterized his prophetic ministry all his years was the ministry of intercession. He was not known as much for his prophetic messages as he was for his prayers. He had learned to instinctively look to God for wisdom and direction. Out of habitual communion with the Holy One of Israel, he was able to be God's man and voice to a stubborn people—all because prayer had become his vital breath and native air.

Let us now note some recorded occasions in which Samuel prayed.

Samuel Prayed for Deliverance

Having grown weary of their Philistine oppressors, Israel complained to the Lord and the Lord spoke to Samuel and Samuel spoke to the people: "Gather all Israel to Mizpah and I will pray to the Lord for you" (1 Sam. 7:5). Then upon gathering, the people said to Samuel, "Do not cease to cry to the LORD God for us . . ." (1 Sam. 7:8). After offering a sacrifice to the LORD, "Samuel cried to the LORD for Israel and the LORD answered him" (1 Sam. 7:9).

Blessed indeed are those people who have a leader of the quality of a Samuel to intercede for them — men and women who wrestle before the throne of grace for God's mercy to be poured out on their church, or ministry, or some particular situation. How often churches and ministries languish in despair because no one is standing in the gap to cry out to God for them. "I searched for a man among them who would build up the wall and stand in the gap before Me for the land, so that I would not destroy it; but I found no one" (Ezek. 22:30). This is not to suggest that every situation can be changed by the prayers of godly praying people — both biblical history and experience testifies otherwise — but surely God would like to bare his arm among us more often than what many of our churches are experiencing.

Samuel knew God and the people knew that he knew God. And he got his prayers answered. So effective were his prayers that the Bible reports, "And the hand of the LORD was against the Philistines all the days of Samuel" (1 Sam. 7:13).

Samuel Prayed for God's Choice

Although it was neither God's nor Samuel's preference for Israel to have a king other than Yahweh himself, the Lord accommodated Israel and granted their desire to have a human leader like the surrounding nations. It was out of the prophet's quiet time with his Lord, that the Lord revealed to Samuel that a man by the name of Saul was to be Israel's first king. "Now a day before Saul's coming, the LORD revealed this to Samuel saying, 'About this time tomorrow I will send a man from the land of Benjamin, and you shall anoint him to be prince over My people Israel . . .'" (1 Sam. 9:15).

We are living in such a different and desperate church age now. When I was called to my first church fresh out of Bible College, the tried and tested pastoral candidating policy for a local church board was to make inquiry of a few godly leaders who knew the candidate, and whose wisdom they valued, then to take their recommendation before the Lord and seriously pray over it.

But what is the situation today? The corporate world has walked through the church's front door into the *boardroom*. As many boards review one *polished*, inflated pastoral candidate's résumé after another, what are they looking for? Too often it is for a suave corporate ecclesiastical executive to run a smooth religious organization; a charismatic personality who is expert in carrying water on both shoulders; a sermonizer who promises that his sermonettes won't exceed fifteen minutes!

I would like to hear of a church board who has the courage to break the mold. Let them get down on their knees and wait on God until they receive God's wisdom regarding his choice.

Things have gotten out of hand. Yes, I think we ought to be skeptical about the person who is forever saying, "The Lord showed me" and "The Lord told me." On the other hand, I think a board would do well in its search for their next pastor, to bring before it a few of its parishioners, who are reputed to be godly people, and ask for their prayerful counsel. Let's throw the worldly, corporate paradigm out and bring God's ways back!

Even though Samuel's prayers didn't keep King Saul from failure, yet they were effectual in providing Israel with God's chosen man. Can't God do the same for us in our own day? For your church? For your ministry? In our time? I believe he can and will if we seek his ways.

Samuel Prayed for a Fallen Leader

Upon hearing from God that Saul's pride had caused him to disobey God and precipitate a disastrous defeat for Israel, "Samuel cried out to the LORD all night (1 Sam. 15:1).

This prophet often cried out to God. I heard a pastor say in a sermon recently that the Lord had spoken to him about his failure to cry out to him for his people. He said he hadn't quit praying for his people, but that his intercessions had become too routine, too monotonous. The Lord told him to start crying out to him.

If language means anything, this language of crying out to God means that the intercessor's heart and voice become so engaged about a matter that inaudible praying, or quiet praying, won't do.

You can rest assured that Samuel didn't cry out to God in a church office at nine o'clock in the morning with his administrative assistant sitting in the next room. People and pastors who cry out to God get off alone by themselves—just themselves and God. They don't want anyone within earshot. These matters are too sacred to be overheard by anyone. In this case, a leader had fallen and a man who cared about his people and the leader spent the night on his face before God. He cried—and he cried out. He wept; he agonized; he grieved; he was in deep pain and anguish of soul. The man he had anointed to be Israel's king had fallen—and God had just told the prophet that he now regretted ever placing him over his people. The prophet hurt for the king; he hurt for the people; he hurt for God.

The Church Needs More Samuels

Answers to our prayers do not come with a guarantee. Just because God gave us a certain leader in answer to prayer does not mean that person will always be God's person for that place for all time. People fail, leaders fall—but God's work goes on. Thus, God turns to Samuel and says, "How long will you grieve over Saul, since I have rejected him from being king over Israel? Fill your horn with oil and go; I will send you to Jesse the Bethlehemite, for I have selected a king for Myself among his sons" (1 Sam. 16:1). Once again, as a result of prayerful communion with God, Samuel is told who Israel's next leader is to be.

Israel was blessed to have been given such a man as Samuel to pray for them. May the same God be pleased in our day to raise up many after his kind in the Church. We are desperately in need of praying people—praying prophets—men and women who will pray for God to intervene, to give deliverance; people who will pray for God's choice for leadership. *O Lord, give us in our own day such people!*

We need a few men and women, who may be quite ordinary and yet exceptional like Thomas Haire, who became known as the praying plumber from Lisburn, Ireland. Haire once said to A. W. Tozer (1897-1963), "Praying is working along with God in the fulfillment of the divine plan. Praying is fighting close up front where the sharp deciding action is taking place. Prayer takes into account what the devil is trying to accomplish and where he is working, and attacks him at that strategic point."[2]

Samuel was that kind of intercessor; he was that kind of prophet. He was a praying prophet. May God in his mercy be pleased to give the church more praying Samuels.

Called by God when but a mere child,
he learned to discern his Father's clear voice.
"Speak, Lord, for your servant is listening,"
was his lifelong habit from a loving choice.

CHAPTER 17

The "Ifs" of Jesus

The ways of God with men are marvelous indeed. This is seen again and again as we read the Word of God and observe the life and ministry of the Lord Jesus.

As Creator, our God has put in place specific laws which he actively uses to perpetuate and sustain this wonderful universe. In creating the vegetable kingdom, God established a *natural* law in order that each specie would reproduce itself after its own kind (see Gen. 1)· For example, whenever a farmer plants wheat in the spring, he can expect to harvest wheat in the fall. He doesn't plant wheat seed and subsequently reap soybeans. Why is that? Because of the divinely established laws of reproduction. God says in essence, "If you plant wheat, you will reap wheat." God made it so.

God has also put into motion laws, or principles, whereby he actively works in the lives of his children. For example, one cannot read the Gospel accounts without being struck by the "If Sayings" of Jesus. By "If Sayings," I mean those sayings of Jesus which he introduced with an "if" clause.

Jesus taught that spiritual blessings and fruitful discipleship are *conditional*. He shared this teaching in a multiplicity of settings, with various audiences. Our Lord taught his hearers repeatedly that the Father works among men according to the law of condition and promise. This law—a principle of condition and consequence—is invariable. If we meet certain conditions, God has obligated himself to respond in a specific way.

I realize there are many earnest Christians who have a different view of God's sovereignty. Many of these well-intentioned people believe that man plays merely a passive role in his and her salvation. I believe God has said otherwise.

While nothing man does gains *merit* with God or *meritoriously* contributes to his justification: "For by grace you have been saved through faith. And this is not your own doing; it is the gift of God, [9] not a result of works, so that no one may boast" (Eph. 2:8); yet man is neither a passive bystander in either regenerating or sanctifying graces. The cooperation of our wills, graciously acted upon and energized by a merciful God, is necessary in both raising us from our spiritual graves and conforming us to the likeness of God's dear Son.

In speaking of the "cooperation of our wills," I'm not suggesting that we exercise our wills apart from the grace of God. No, a thousand times no! An example of the *balance* between God's saving initiative and grace, and the human response of our will is found in Philippians 2:12-13: "work out your own salvation, with fear and trembling, for it is God who works in you both to will and to work for his good pleasure."[1] As God "works" in us, we are to "work out" our response.

While God is free to do as he chooses, he is also free to establish ways by which he exercises his freedom. This he has done in establishing the *laws of condition and promise*. God has chosen to operate in the life of the individual disciple and in the corporate life of Christ's church, according to the principles he has ordained.

I want us now to consider three of these "If Sayings " of Jesus as they relate to the individual follower of the Lord Jesus; they are recorded in the Gospel of John. Clearly, each of these sayings of Jesus are meant to be universally applicable in every age and for every believer, who meets the respective conditions.

The "If" of Soul-Thirst

"If anyone thirsts, let him come to me and drink. Whoever believes in me, as the Scripture has said, 'Out of his heart will flow rivers of living water'" (John 7:37-38).

The occasion on which Jesus spoke these words was the Jewish Feast of Tabernacles. Thousands of worshipers gathered annually in

Jerusalem in the month of either September or October, to celebrate the harvest and offer thanks to God. This festive event memorialized Israel's journey from Egypt to Canaan, and served as a reminder of God's benevolent provision during tough times.

Each day of the feast, at the time of the morning sacrifice, a priest brought into the forecourt of the temple a golden vessel, filled with water drawn from the springs of Shiloh. The water was poured — mingled with sacrificial wine — into two bowls which stood upon the altar. During this sacred rite, the priests sounded trumpets, clashed symbols, and then the words of Isaiah 12:3 were recited: "With joy you will draw water from the wells of salvation."

This feast lasted for seven days, with a closing assembly on the eighth day, "the great day" (John 7:37). It was on this day the Lord Jesus was compelled by the Spirit to make such a startling prophetic announcement. He promised that when the age of the Spirit was inaugurated (see John 7:39), it would be the privilege of every thirsty-hearted disciple to become a *cataract of blessing*.

Where is the person born of the Spirit of God, who does not desire to live a life of effective fruitfulness to the glory of God? Surely every believer reading these words has such aspirations. Take heart, hungry Christian! These words of Jesus hold the key to a life of fruitful service.

Jesus says that "rivers of living water" will flow from the depths of one's inner being ("heart") on one condition — an intense soul-thirst that draws a person to the Lord Jesus.

Excuse the grammar lesson, but the Greek grammatical tenses and moods are revealing in this text: "thirsts," is a present subjunctive; "let him come," is a present middle imperative; "drink," is in the present imperfect tense; "believes," is a present participle. The text, in keeping with the tenses and moods, could be rendered to read: "*If anyone thirsts, let him come to me and drink and keep on drinking. Whoever constantly believes in me, as the Scripture has said, 'Out of his heart will flow rivers of living water.'*"

The annuals of the church have proven the words of our Lord to be true, time without number. Wherever there has been a thirsty-hearted follower of the Man with the Golden Pitcher, there has been an infusion of the Holy Spirit and a consequent effusion of power and fruitfulness. All this is contingent upon a soul-thirst, graciously given by a merciful God, which pours itself out in strong faith to our welcoming Mediator at the Father's right hand.

The question is: Are you *thirsty*? Am I *thirsty*? Jesus assures us "if" we are authentically craving him, are constantly drawing from him, our life will be a channel of fruitfulness and blessing.

The "If" of Discipleship

"If anyone serves me, he must follow me; and where I am, there will my servant be also. If anyone serves me, the Father will honor him" (John 12:26).

These words have been resonating in my spirit for many months now. I have been a servant of the Lord Jesus for over fifty years—a faulty servant, to be sure; a servant who has not always been perfectly faithful and absolutely obedient—nevertheless, a servant. More than once my Father in Heaven has taken me into his "woodshed," chastising his careless son for attitudes and actions unbecoming one of his followers. Yet, because of his merciful, preserving grace, I have never left—nor wanted to—Christ's School of Discipleship from the day I first enrolled. (If there are others who can honestly testify to a lengthy pilgrimage of uninterrupted fellowship with our Father in Heaven, I commend them and the grace of God. For me, I would be less than honest if I made such a claim.) Regrettably, but thankfully, I know what it is to feel my Father's rod of discipline.

Often my merciful Lord has led me through bitter tears of regret and repentance. And this is what I have learned, and am learning, through these anguishing experiences: this life with Christ is a relationship, a walk, a fellowship. It is not given in the form of a "package"—in one fell-swoop. It is dynamic by nature, not static. This life, this relationship, must be cultivated and nurtured. If left untended, our Lord will grievously walk away into the shadows, like a wounded lover. But if tended, this love relationship will develop into a spiritual romance not unlike Solomon and his bride (see Song of Solomon).

The Christian is called to be a slave of the Lord Jesus Christ. This suggests that he has voluntarily submitted himself, and all that he is and has, to be a faithful love-slave of the King of kings and Lord of lords. This is not a servile, slavish task. It is a calling, the highest of privileges.

The master Teacher knew there would always be those who would nominally identify with him and his teaching, but who rejected his lordship over them. The courageous Lutheran pastor-theologian, Dietrich Bonhoeffer (1906-1945), called this "cheap grace" — a kind of grace which is divorced from a corresponding obedience to Christ.

Living four hundred years after the founder of the Reformation movement, Bonhoeffer witnessed firsthand the absence of a living faith among the religious throng. As a voice in the wilderness, this man who would soon be martyred at the hands of Nazi despots, challenged the church of his day: "When he spoke of grace, Luther always implied as a corollary that it cost him his own life, the life which was now for the first time subjected to the absolute obedience to Christ." Then Bonhoeffer pronounced this indictment, which could be applied to much of the church of our own day: "Judged by the standard of Luther's doctrine, that of his followers was unassailable, and yet their orthodoxy spelt the end and destruction of the Reformation as a revelation on earth of the costly grace of God. *The justification of the sinner in the world degenerated into the justification of sin and the world. Costly grace was turned into cheap grace without discipleship.*"[2]

Nineteen hundred years before Bonehoeffer wrote those words, our Lord joined grace and obedience, justification and sanctification, faith and discipleship: "If anyone serves me, let him follow me . . ."[3] In other words, for every person wishing to be, or professing to be, a servant of Jesus, our Lord says following him is not optional. Obedience is inherent in discipleship. These words were spoken by our Lord to inquiring "Greeks." Having spoken to Philip, a disciple of the Lord Christ, about their desire for a personal audience with Jesus ("Sir, we wish to see Jesus."), by his response, Jesus made certain these men should be under no illusions as to what was involved in identifying with him. It meant a death to and abandonment of the *self-life*. To Jesus, discipleship is "a long road of obedience in the same direction," as Eugene Petersen calls it.[4] There is no other way; there are no shortcuts to discipleship. Discipleship is *followership* — following Jesus. To such faithful, obedient followers, Christ assures us the Father will bestow "honor." What a privilege to be a follower of Jesus!

The "If" of Faith

"Jesus said to her, 'Did I not tell you that if you believed you would see the glory of God?'" (John 11:40).

Lazarus, a friend of Jesus, and a brother of Mary and Martha, was dead. Both sisters had enough confidence in Jesus that had he been present when their brother became seriously ill, Jesus could have healed him (see John 11:21, 32). However, they did not have faith that Jesus could raise Lazarus from death.

Jesus had previously assured Martha that her brother would rise again (John 11:23). But she took that to mean at the last resurrection. Martha believed that Jesus was the promised Messiah and the Son of God (John 11:27), but she had no confidence that he could do what all thought to be impossible — raise the dead in the here and now.

Our Lord assured Martha that the "glory of God" would be revealed if she only believed. As used in this context, the "glory of God" means a demonstration of God's power, a God-event; it is a supernatural operation of the Spirit of God that is manifested here on earth, to the glory and praise of the Lord Jesus. God's glory cannot be dictated or manipulated. When experienced or seen, it changes lives, churches and communities.

Might I stop here long enough to ask, *Is this not one of the Church's crying needs — to see repeated demonstrations of God's glory?* Not the particular miracle which Christ performed outside little Bethany many years ago, but spiritual resurrections and transformations in the lives of those who are dead in trespasses and in sins.

The glory of God — a God-event — cannot be manufactured or programmed. It does not come from below but is sent from above. Man can't produce a God-event. Only *God* can produce God-events. Only God can raise the spiritually dead; only God can make saints out of sinners; only God can breathe life into a corpse; only God can give a "beautiful headdress instead of ashes, the oil of gladness instead of mourning, the garment of praise instead of a faint spirit" (Isa. 61:3).

People will travel long distances to witness a God-event, the glory of God. John informs us later in his Gospel: "When the large crowd of the Jews learned that Jesus was there, they came, not only on account of him but also to see Lazarus, whom he had raised from the dead" (John 11:9). It has been my privilege through the years to personally witness this same glory—God-events—manifesting itself in transformed lives of redeemed sinners. But I want to see so much more. What about you, dear reader?

Jesus tied faith to this particular God-event: "Did I not tell you that if you *believed* you would see the glory of God?" Is our Lord implying that we could see more of the glory of God—God-events—if we actually believed he could perform such? I think so.

There you have it: three pertinent and pungent "ifs" of Jesus: "The 'If' of Soul-Thirst"; "The 'If' of Discipleship"; and "The 'If' of Faith." Would you now join with me in praying that you and I will come to Christ's terms and meet the respective conditions of these truths. Will we allow the Holy Spirit to take Christ's words and make them real to us and in us—today and every day? The Lord Jesus awaits our response.

O God, my gracious Father,
May rivers of blessing flow as I crave You thirstily.
May I serve You by following Your Son unswervingly.
May I see Your glory as I gaze on Christ trustingly.
Amen.

CHAPTER 18

The Apollos Problem

In just the past few weeks, several Christian lay people have shared with me similar stories that, sadly, are all too familiar. The individuals who spoke with me are not cantankerous saints; they don't have a reputation for being difficult people. And each of them has maintained a long-term commitment to his and her respective local churches. For the most part, each has served in a leadership role for many years. What is their similar refrain? It is this: "Our pastor is a wonderful person and he preaches a good sermon, but he does not preach with *power*."

No power! Each of these pastors is seminary trained. Each came to his church highly recommended by church leaders, ministerial colleagues and seminary professors. Each one has devoted hundreds of hours to the study of the Old and New Testament Scriptures. They have meticulously studied the life and ministry of the Lord Jesus Christ. They have read and re-read the Book of Acts. And yet, years later, the complaint of some of the godliest people in the pews is: "Our pastor doesn't preach with power!"

No Holy Spirit power!

How is it that a man can have earned a Bible college or seminary degree and not preach with power? How is it that a man can know the Scriptures from cover to cover and not preach with power? How is it that a preacher can possess oratorical and homiletical skills and not preach with power? How is it that a pastor can have an excellent command of his native tongue, deliver a sermon with appropriate illustrations, and not preach with power?

A Powerless Preacher

The answer? It is found in Acts 18:24-28. This passage is a brief historical account of a preacher by the name of Apollos, who was preaching without the power of the Holy Spirit.[1]

Apollos possessed superb ministerial credentials; Providence was kind to this preacher. Having been born into a Jewish home in the city of Alexandria — a city with a Jewish population of some one million in that day — he was surrounded by expert Torah scholars.[2] Because of his disciplined training, he would later be "useful in convincing the Jews, for he would be able to find Christ all over the Old Testament and to prove to them that the Old Testament looked forward all the time to his coming."[3]

Not only was this man mighty in the Scriptures, he later came to faith in Jesus Christ and was "instructed in the way of the Lord" (Acts 18:25).[4] We don't know anything about the occasion and circumstances surrounding his conversion; however, having been raised and educated in a deeply rich Jewish tradition, his conversion to Christ had to result in much personal suffering.

Following his conversion, Apollos preached with passion, for Luke says he was "fervent in spirit" (Acts 18:25). This Alexandrian educated preacher, preached with great emotional and physical energy, and with firm conviction. His listeners never had to think twice as to whether or not this man was convinced about his subject matter; he enthusiastically communicated his new-found discoveries to all who would listen.

Furthermore, Apollos' preaching didn't lack substance. His sermons were not all *heat* with no *light*. Luke says, "he was speaking and teaching accurately the things concerning Jesus" (Acts 18:25). His was not a zeal without knowledge. No apostle could fault him for not having done his homework (as far as it went). He was convinced that Jesus was the one spoken of by the prophets, and he preached accordingly with all his oratorical eloquence. Apollos would have thrilled the typical Evangelical congregation, as he quoted Old Testament texts from memory: "My, what a preacher!"

Only John's Baptism

But there was something definitively lacking in both Apollos' knowledge and experience. Not everyone detected what it was. But there were two who did. While listening to him, Priscilla and Aquila discerned that this mighty expositor lacked the *power* of the Holy Spirit. Following one of his sermons, this godly husband and wife discreetly approached the preacher and asked for a private audience. They inquired as to Apollos' biblical and experiential knowledge. He acknowledged that he was "acquainted only with the baptism of John."

"*Only* with the baptism of John!" When this Spirit-filled couple heard that, they knew they had their answer. Apollos had been baptized with water but was not "clothed with power from on high" (Luke 24:49). What were Priscilla and Aquila to do? Luke says they "explained to him the way of God more accurately" (Acts 18:26). And what was the result? He was filled with the Holy Spirit. How do we know that? Because of the larger context. In the very next chapter we have Paul coming into Ephesus and finding some followers of Christ. One of the first questions he put to these converts was, "Did you receive the Holy Spirit when [it can also be translated "since"] you believed?" (Acts 19:2). What was their answer? "No" (Acts 19:2). Then Paul asked these Ephesians, "Into what then were you baptized?" Their answer? The same answer Apollos gave to Priscilla and Aquila: "Into John's baptism" (Acts 19:3).

To those who might argue: "Yes, but since the Ephesians had only experienced John's baptism, Paul went ahead and baptized them with water in the name of Jesus—and that's what they lacked." But that's only half of the story. Acts 19:6 reads, "the Holy Spirit came upon them." As necessary as water baptism is, all the water in the world will not enable a preacher to preach in the power of the Holy Spirit. It was the original Water Baptizer himself—John the Baptist—who announced, "As for me, I baptize you with water for repentance, but He who is coming after me . . . He will baptize you with the Holy Spirit and fire" (Matt. 3:11).

The sad fact of the matter is, that most preachers and Christians have only experienced one baptism—water baptism. They have never experienced the Spirit coming *upon* them (Acts 19:6). They have never been endued with "power from on high."

I can almost hear someone remonstrate: *I believe all Christians are baptized with the Holy Spirit at the point of their conversion, when they first trusted in Christ.* Granted, every person born from above does receive the Spirit of adoption and is enabled to call God his Father (see Rom. 8:15). Every Christian is indwelt by the Holy Spirit (see Rom. 8:9). And all Christians have been baptized into the body of Christ—the Church of the living God (see 1 Cor. 12:13). But not all Christians have been "clothed with power." Not all Christians have been filled with the Spirit. Not all Christians have experienced the Spirit's coming upon them. If this were the case, *all* preachers would be preaching in the power of the Spirit, *all* Christians would be walking in the power of the Spirit, and *all* of our churches would be enjoying apostolic fruit. But let's be candid: this simply is not true to the facts. And why not? Possibly because of our doctrinal prejudices; or because of uninformed pastors and preachers; or because our fleshly tendencies prevent us from seeing the reality of this biblical truth and experience.

Some are so prejudiced against any message or ministry that honors the Holy Spirit that they are grieving the Spirit. Some are so afraid of fanaticism and emotionalism—as I am, too—that they sleepily embrace a kind of sterile, metallic brand of Christianity that is powerless to raise a spiritually dead Lazarus.

There are some biblical terms which carry with them a stigma in many of our church circles: words like "Pentecost," "filled with the Spirit," "gifts of the Spirit," "holiness," "power in the Spirit," —even "Spirit" or "Holy Spirit." These words are avoided like the plague.

And could it be that they are avoided because such individuals have never experienced a mighty baptism with the Holy Spirit? I think so.

Our Greatest Need

The church has relied too long upon academic credentials, ecclesiastical machinery, and the efforts and ingenuity of the flesh instead of the blessed Holy Spirit. And the results? A skilled, professional clergy who know *only* John's baptism. And since the pastor cannot lead his people where he himself has not traveled, our pews are populated for the most part with sincere people who may have been born from above, but who know nothing of the power of the Holy Spirit in their own lives.

I'm convinced that most churches are content to have an Apollos as their preacher — one who has never been "clothed with power from on high"; one who never preaches in the power of the Spirit. Why do I say that? Because — and let's be candid here — this is the present pathetic state of the average church. There is a famine of Spirit-filled preachers. I say this with an aching heart. I don't delight in writing this.

What is our greatest lack? The Holy Spirit. What is our greatest need? The Holy Spirit. Who is the missing Presence? The Holy Spirit. Oh, for preachers like the venerable Baptist, Charles Spurgeon (1834-1892), who when ascending to his pulpit every Sunday morning and evening, prayed at each of the fifteen steps, "Come, Holy Spirit." Is it any wonder the Lord honored his ministry with much fruit as he preached in the power of the Spirit to London's masses?

The saintly English Methodist, Samuel Chadwick (1860-1932), in writing on this subject said, "Pentecost transforms the preacher. The commonest bush ablaze with the presence of God becomes a miracle of glory. . . . Indifference to religion is impossible where the preacher is a flame of fire. . . . The only power that is adequate for Christian life and Christian work is the power of the Holy Spirit."[5]

Listen to what Martyn Lloyd-Jones (1899-1981), the late renowned pastor of London's Westminster Chapel, had to say on this subject:

> The church has fallen into the error of thinking that a man can get this knowledge by academic teaching and learning. I am not here to decry these things; [he was a medical doctor when God called him to preach]. . . . But they are not all-important, and the tragedy of the last hundred years has been to put a premium on such things, men boasting of their degrees and diplomas . . . and so on. That is all very well, but it is not the way to know God more fully. *It is through the Spirit, through the baptism of the Spirit that one comes to this fuller knowledge.*[5]

Thomas Aquinas (1225-1274) was one of the Roman Catholic Church's greatest theologians. In 1879 the Pope officially proclaimed him to be, in effect, the theologian and teacher of the entire "Holy Catholic Church." His famous theological work. *The Summa Theologica,* has been regarded ever since the twelfth century the standard work of the Roman Catholic Church. Aquinas was regarded as one of the greatest thinkers and philosophers. And yet, he taught that it was impossible for a mortal man to have any kind of direct experience with God. After spending his entire life teaching that man could have no contact with immaterial reality, shortly before his death he had such an overwhelming experience of God that he could write no more theology. In responding to a friend who urged him to finish his great work, *The Summa Theologica,* he replied, "I can do no more; such things have been revealed to me that all that I have written seems as straw, and I now await the end of my life."[6]

Amazing! Here was a man who had written volumes of theology and was recognized by his church as being its foremost theologian and teacher, but upon having a personal divine encounter with the Spirit of God, he laid his pen aside saying that everything prior to this experience was like "straw"!

Thus it will be with the man who has experienced what Apollos did, after being carefully instructed by two Spirit-filled lay people, Priscilla and Aquila. All he has ever preached and done before will seem like nothing but "straw" after he has been filled with the Holy Spirit. Ask the apostles Peter and Paul if this is not so. Ask George Whitefield and John Wesley if this is not so. Ask D. L. Moody and Blaise Pascal if this is not so. Ask Evan Roberts and Robert Murray M'Cheyne if this is not so. Ask A. W. Tozer, A. B. Simpson, A. J. Gordon and Martyn Lloyd-Jones — as well as a myriad of lesser lights, if this is not so.

It is so. The New Testament affirms, and a host of thirsty-hearted men and women can testify to the reality of the blessed experience of being "clothed from on high." No denomination or movement has sole ownership as to the truth of this experience. The halls of church history are replete with Baptists and Mennonites, Anglicans and Presbyterians, Methodists and Wesleyans, Lutherans and Nazarenes — men and women who finally tired of living a powerless life and were led into a life of power in the Holy Spirit.

Dwight Lyman Moody (1837-1899), also known as D. L. Moody, was an American pastor and evangelist who founded the Moody Church (Chicago), Northfield School, and Mount Hermon School in Massachusetts, the Moody Bible Institute and Moody Publishers. Though many would have thought this converted shoe salesman was quite successful as a pastor in the early years of his ministry, there were two saintly ladies who discerned a noticeable lack in this zealot for Christ. I'll allow his biographers to tell the story.

> Occasionally after some of his meetings in Chicago, two Free Methodist women would say to him, "Mr. Moody, we are praying that you may receive the enduement of the Holy Spirit." This irritated Moody who believed they should rather pray for the people. But they persistently prayed that he would "get the power." Moody did not know exactly what they meant. Finally won over by their godly concern, he asked them to show him in the Scriptures the truth they insisted upon, and he even prayed with them for this power.
>
> Over months, as Moody gave himself to prayer, he realized the state his heart was in. "I found I was ambitious; I was not preaching Christ; I was preaching for ambition. I found everything in my heart that ought not be there. For four months, a wrestling went on within me, and I was a miserable man."[1]
>
> The anointing for which he prayed finally came when Moody was on a trip to New York to raise money after the Chicago Fire. One day while he walked along Wall Street, Moody was so overcome with God's love that he had to find a friend's home to get alone to pray. The sense of God's presence was so great that he asked the Lord to withhold His hand lest he die on the spot. The experience, Moody later said, marked a turning point in his life. From then on he didn't preach differently but the response was greater than ever before.
>
> How did Moody refer to this experience? He spoke of it as "a gift of the Holy Spirit for service," "a filling," "an anointing," "an unction," "an empowering for service," and "a baptism of the Holy Spirit." What mattered was not the

name, but the reality of it.[7]

The Apollos problem is not only a *preacher* problem — it is a *pew* problem as well. However, God has called preachers to lead the way. But where they don't, blessed is that preacher who has a discreet Priscilla and Aquila who will humbly show him the way.

No power? Try Pentecost!

He once was a mighty orator,
  quoting the Scriptures at will.
He preached the words of Jesus the Christ,
  Amazing listeners with skill.
But a knowing couple saw his lack,
  taking the preacher aside.
They explained God's ways more perfectly,
  So that his fruit might abide.

CHAPTER 19

Living a Focused Life

Too many Christians are living life without focus. They resemble the blind man, who when asked by Jesus what he saw after the Master had touched his eyes, replied, "I see men, but they look like trees, walking." He saw, but everything was distorted, out of focus. Following Christ's second touch "he saw everything clearly" (see Mark 8:22-26).[1]

To change metaphors, these living-without-focus Christians are like sleepwalkers, bumping into "walls" and stumbling down "stairs," with no sense of direction or purpose. Many of them are running at a feverish pace, but have no idea where they're going.

They remind me of an incident that happened to Thomas Huxley one day. A devoted disciple of Darwin and a self-avowed humanist, Huxley had just finished delivering a series of lectures. Taking one of Dublin's horse-drawn taxis, he assumed the driver had been told what his destination was. Upon entering the taxi, all he had told the driver was, "Hurry, I'm almost late. Drive fast!" Before long Huxley discovered the carriage was headed in the wrong direction. He shouted to the driver, "Do you know where you're going?" Without looking back, the driver yelled, "No, your honor! But I'm driving very fast!"

Yes, we're driving very fast, but haven't stopped to consider what our objectives are, our goals, our destination.

The devout Christian and Quaker Thomas Kelly (1893-1941) once observed, "The outer distractions of our interests reflect an inner lack of integration in our own selves. We are trying to be several selves at once without all our selves being organized by a single, mastering Life within us."[2]

These are arresting words, spoken by a man who did more than write. He thought. He pondered. He meditated. Then he wrote. And he wrote because he had something to say. Can we say that we are "being organized by a single, mastering Life within us"?

Living in the dawn of this very modern twenty-first century, we Christians are besieged with continuing multiple choices. It can be overwhelming. Of course, the individual choices we make will impact our personal spiritual growth, our families, our church, our community — even destinies. It's important that we make the right decisions at critical intervals. But it won't be easy.

Addressing this great pressure the modern world exerts on the Christian, evangelical author and conference speaker Os Guinness writes, that unless believers learn to cope successfully with what he terms "pluralization," we cannot expect to live the Christian life successfully with confidence. Guinness defines pluralization as "the process by which the proliferation of choice rapidly multiplies the number of options." He goes on to say, "This affects the private sphere of modern society at all levels, from consumer goods to relationships to worldviews and faiths."[3]

We are not the only ones who have faced a myriad of daily and weekly options. Although our age may be technologically astute, our Lord and first-century Christians also had to make choices. How did Jesus and these ancient believers manage to live an abundant life, anyway? Why did they decide to do the things that they did? What was their motivation?

Living with a Sense of Calling

One need never question whether or not the Lord Jesus ever lived a focused life. From the day he announced to his concerned parents, "Did you not know that I must be in my Father's house?" (Luke 2:49), to the day he cried from the cross, "It is finished!" (John 19:30), Jesus lived his days and nights with a sense of calling.

Our Lord knew who he was, where he had come from, why he

was here, what he was to do while here, and where he was going. He was commissioned and on a mission. He allowed nothing and no one to distract or deter him. By the Spirit's power, filling and guidance, Jesus overcame temptation, kept to his Father's priorities, and faithfully stayed the course despite deserting disciples and religious fanatics. Neither governments nor councils could dissuade him from accomplishing his mission. Myopic disciples and faithless followers were not allowed to interfere with his calling. His ear was tuned to the beat of the Silent Drummer. He was called. He would be faithful.

The Christian is not to live a *driven* life. The Christian is to live a *called* life. Of this the early Christians were persuaded. Thus Paul wrote to the Romans: "Paul, a servant of Christ Jesus, *called* to be an apostle" (Rom. 1:1, emphasis added). Again to the Corinthians: Paul, *called* by the will of God to be an apostle" (1 Cor. 1:1, emphasis added). To the Galatians he wrote the same thing in different words: "Paul, an apostle — not from men nor through man, but through Jesus Christ and God the Father" (Gal. 1:1, emphasis added). To the Christians at Rome, Paul reminds them they are "*called* to belong to Jesus Christ," and that they are "*called* to be saints" (Rom. 1:6, 7, emphasis added). Many more references like these on the subject of *calling* could be cited.

All Christians are called by God in the sense of Romans 1:6-7. We are called to belong to Jesus Christ and to live holy lives. This is your calling and mine. But in addition to this *universal* calling which all Christians receive, there is a *vocational* calling which only some Christians receive. Such was the case with Paul. He was not only called to be an apostle, but also a preacher and teacher (see 2:Tim. 1:11).

It is only through experiencing the indwelling Christ and understanding our respective callings, that the Christian will be able to live his or her life with poise and purpose, confidence and quietude.

Our Lord could pray in his final days to the Father, "I glorified you on earth, having accomplished the work that you gave me to do" (John 17:4), because he lived his entire thirty-three years knowing he was called to perform a special mission. What about you and me, my friend? Are we living life with a true knowledge of our calling? If so, we're living a focused life. And by living this kind of life, we discover we just can't do *everything*.

The Discipline of Elimination

Neither the Lord Jesus Christ, the Apostles, nor the first-century Christians could live a focused life without eliminating everything and anything that might hinder their calling and focus. Thus Jesus warned his followers: "If your hand or your foot causes you to sin, cut it off and throw it away. It is better for you to enter life maimed or crippled than to have two hands or two feet and be thrown into eternal fire. And if your eye causes you to sin, gouge it out and throw it away. It is better for you to enter life with one eye than to have two eyes and be thrown into the fire of hell" (Matt. 18:8-9).

Again, concerned with the fleshly impediments that he knew would prevent them from growing in the grace and knowledge of God as they should, the inspired writer of the book of Hebrews wrote these words to languishing believers: "let us lay aside every weight, and the sin which clings so closely" (Heb. 12:1).

I well remember hearing the news as a young boy in 1954, that the four-minute mile barrier had been broken. Olympic runner Roger Bannister broke the tape in record time — 3:59.4. How did he do it? Just as every other successful athlete competes successfully: by eliminating everything that kept him from his calling and goal. One can't go everywhere, do everything, enjoy every food, stay up all hours of the night, and set a record like Bannister did.

Jerome (342-420) was a master of classical learning — his age's best Latin writer, some have said. He had a passion for scholarship and devoured the works of pagan thinkers. As a Christian, Jerome was troubled by his failure to implement healthy priorities. Historians say that he preferred the cultured style of Cicero and other rhetoricians to the plain, and — what he considered to be — clumsy style of the language of the Bible.

But a transforming event changed Jerome. One historian records: "In Antioch he had a feverish dream in which Christ scourged him and accused him, 'You are a Ciceronian, and not a Christian.' Jerome vowed not to study pagan books again."[4]

Let's face it: We cannot live a focused life and fulfill our calling if we allow our inner and outer lives to fill up with moral junk and clutter. Either we get rid of the junk or the junk will eventually extinguish our light and neutralize our fruitfulness and effectiveness. We have a choice.

An Unswerving Commitment

To be called, and to be committed to our calling, are not synonymous. The shores of time are strewn with faithless Christians who failed to pursue a godly lifestyle, or who quit his or her vocational callings. Of the one, Jesus said: "No one, after putting his hand to the plow and looking back, is fit for the kingdom of God" (Luke 9:62 NASB). Of the other, the apostle Paul wrote: "Demas, having loved this present world, has deserted me " (2 Tim. 4:10 NASB).

One cannot stay true to his calling without remaining passionately in love with the Lord Jesus Christ. When our love for Christ grows cold, our faithfulness to Christ and our calling grow dim — and eventually will die if we aren't renewed by the Spirit. Only by staying at the foot of the Cross are we safe. A passion for Jesus makes all the difference. And that passion must be fed.

A careless, passionate Christian is an oxymoron. One cannot live a careless Christian life and be totally committed to Christ. Too many Christians are living a double-minded life. They're neither comfortable in the world nor in the church. And they're a spiritual drag on both.

Wake up, Christian! It could be the world, the flesh and the Devil have anesthetized you! Don't you hear the Lord Jesus saying, "Behold, I am coming like a thief! Blessed is the one who stays awake, keeping his garments on, that he may not go about naked and be seen exposed" (Rev. 16:15).

Are you "looking back"? Have you fallen in love with the world? As a teenager, helping my brother-in-law Joe on his farm, I well remember how he first taught me to plow a straight furrow with the tractor. Going out into a large field in springtime, he told me to point the front of the tractor at a distant object. By keeping the tractor on that object I would be able to plow the first furrow straight, thereby assuring all the others would be straight as well.

Being the young kid that I was, I remember after Joe left me to myself, experimenting. I thought to myself while plowing that first furrow, *I had better look behind me occasionally to see how it's going.* Well, as I'm sure you know, every time I looked back, I created a "dogleg" in that furrow.

Jesus knew about farming and he knew people. He knew his followers could not live a successful Christian life while looking back — back to Sodom, back at the world. What about you, my friend? Are you totally surrendered to the Lord Jesus Christ? Totally? Or are you looking back? You have a choice, you know. You will never fulfill your universal calling — to belong to Jesus Christ — or your spiritual vocational calling, whatever that may be — without making and maintaining a total surrender to our Lord and Teacher.

Dependence on the Holy Spirit

Maybe you haven't heard of Charlie Riggs (1916-2008). Charlie served for many years as the crusade director for Billy Graham. He got the job in 1952 on the eve of the famous New York City crusade at Madison Square Garden when the director had to be replaced.

Billy Graham later said of Charlie, "I didn't think he could do it. But I had this peace — that Charlie so depended on the Holy Spirit that I knew the Lord could do it through Charlie."

Charlie had little formal training. When asked how he was able to handle the crusade logistics so well and for so many years, he said with typical humility, "I always asked the Lord to put me in over my head. That way, when I had a job to do, either the Lord had to help me or I was sunk." God was delighted to help Charlie again and again.[5]

To live a focused life is to live a life of total dependence on the Holy Spirit. It is to distrust the flesh. It is to strive to live a life of reverent obedience to the glory and praise of the Lord Jesus Christ.

We can't do this on our own — that's why we are to live in dependence on him. But if we will die — die to ourselves, die to our selfish pursuits and dreams, die to living life on our own terms, die to insisting on our own rights, die to our prideful ways and follies, die to the "I" that controls our life, then we can rise — rise with the very Life that brought the Lord Jesus out of the grave two thousand years ago. Then we will know something about what Thomas Kelly wrote. We will live "by a single, mastering Life within us." In the words of Jesus: "Truly, truly, I say to you, unless a grain of wheat falls into the earth and dies, it remains alone; but if it dies, it bears much fruit.

Whoever loves his life loses it, and whoever hates his life in this world will keep it for eternal life. If anyone serves me, he must follow me; and where I am, there will my servant be also. If anyone serves me, the Father will honor him" (John 12:24-26).

These are three of the open secrets to living a focused Christian life — the Christ-life. Will you join me on this pilgrimage, as we daily, in the power of the Holy Spirit, seek to live up to our callings?

> *I want to live each day remembering*
>   *I'm called to a holy calling —*
> *Eliminating each thing from my life*
>   *That impedes the race I'm running.*
> *All the while gazing on the Lord Jesus,*
>   *My Savior and Encourager.*

CHAPTER 20

Reflecting Christ's Image

The Christian's *premier* model for holy living is neither an apostle nor a church father, neither a reformer nor a revivalist, neither a prophet nor a pastor. Rather, our foremost exemplar for living the Christian life is the Lord Jesus Christ himself.

While the believer has been providentially granted a host of saintly worthies—from biblical times to the present day—who have characteristically demonstrated a heart for God, none of these fallen individuals had, or has, the sinless credentials to qualify as our perfect role model. Only he who walked a flawless life among sinful men qualifies as our infallible standard for holy living.

The Christian has been called by God to be conformed to the likeness of the Lord Jesus: "For those whom He foreknew, he also predestined to become conformed to the image of his Son . . ." (Rom. 8:29).[1] What was Jesus like? How did he act and react? Which of his Son-of-Man attributes are we expected to emulate? While we can't be exhaustive here, let's look at a few ways the Christian is called to be like Jesus, to reflect his image.

Gratitude

Whether it was on the mountainside, looking up to his Father with bread and fish in his hands, or in a cemetery, about to raise his friend from the dead, the characteristic language of Jesus was "Father, I thank you" (John 11:41).

The Christian can be grateful in every circumstánce of life because of his view of the sovereignty of God. He realizes that nothing comes to the God-lover but what has first passed through the counsel of his wise and good Father (see Rom. 8:28). Through temptations or tests, friendly or unfriendly providences, the voluntary and often involuntary language of the mature heart and lips, has come, "Father, I thank you."

There will be occasions when it will be expressed with tears coursing down one's cheeks; and there will be times when it takes some effort to give thanks. Nevertheless, the seasoned believer has learned that God does all things well; therefore, it is the delight of his soul to be thankful in all things: "give thanks in all circumstances; for this is the will of God in Christ Jesus for you" (1 Thess. 5:16).

The Christlike person is a grateful person.

Holiness

Jesus lived on this earth as the sinless Son of Man. While all of his followers have sinned and still fail, they are also *all* called to a holy life.

In his intercession for all his disciples, Christ prayed, "For their sakes I sanctify Myself, that they themselves also may be sanctified in truth" (John 17:19). The biblical meaning of sanctification involves being *set apart* from sin to live wholly for God, as well as inner, *heart* purity.

Since the sinless Son of God had no guilt or inherent sin to be cleansed from, the meaning of his prayer is that he had decisively separated himself from everything that would contaminate his life, so that his followers might be empowered to draw upon his grace to walk a holy walk.

Despite what some well-intentioned people advocate, the Christian will never in this life *flawlessly* reflect the holiness of Christ, but neither will he settle for a *sinning* Christian life. The honest, thirsty-hearted disciple of Jesus knows his fallenness like no one else. He glories in the Cross and the righteousness of Christ, but he knowingly distrusts himself and the flesh.

With all their foibles and infirmities, with all their short-comings and disabilities, with all their failures and trespasses, the Christlike aspire to be like Jesus.

Forgiveness

Jesus is our model for forgiveness. Our Teacher not only taught this truth with his lips, but he movingly underscored it with his life during some of his darkest days on earth. What he admonished his disciples to do toward their offenders at least seventy-times-seven, he himself practiced the same toward his executioners: "Father, forgive them" (Luke 23:24).

Since Jesus extended forgiveness to his enemies while dying on the cross, we too are to follow in his steps by forgiving all those who have ever wronged us, regardless of how deeply we may have been wounded.

Forgiveness does not always come easy. It has been more than thirty-five years ago now that I was standing on a church campground following an afternoon service. As I was visiting with two friends, a woman approached us and addressed me in these precise words, "Brother Tilley, are you still living with your wife? I saw you drive out of a motel parking lot the other day." Then she turned and left. But her poisonous inference was obvious.

I told my friends that I had no idea what she was talking about. However, it occurred to me later in the day that she had seen me leave a hotel where I had inquired about a room for some of my family who were planning to visit us.

This woman who had turned against me and left our church, had determined to poison two of my leaders against me in my presence. Gratefully, these men had the highest confidence in their pastor and were not shaken by her slanderous remark.

But how was I to react? Was I angry? Yes. She had done me a great injustice. Could I forgive her? Yes. How? Because I knew that I had been forgiven far more by a merciful God.

We can forgive others because we've been forgiven ourselves. Though Jesus never had to be forgiven, yet he forgave. What a model he is for us!

Humility

We are exhorted by the Apostle Paul to "Be completely humble" (Eph. 4:2 NIV). In the context of this exhortation, Paul is address-ing the need among the Ephesian Christians to express gentleness, patience and forbearance toward each other, as well as stressing the importance of believers living in harmony and peace with one anoth-er. Knowing that none of these Christian virtues can be practiced without the essential grace of humility, the apostle urges believers to be "completely humble."

One can appropriately deduce that where there is harshness, im-patience, bitterness and grudges, tension and dissension among brothers and sisters in Christ — there is a substantial absence of Christ-like humility.

We are to always keep our eyes fixed on Jesus, our Model, "who made himself nothing, taking the very nature of a servant, being made in human likeness. And being found in appearance as a man, he humbled himself and became obedient to death-even death on a cross!" (Phil. 2:7-8). Charles Spurgeon (1834-1892) often was known to say, "glance at people; gaze on Jesus." Good advice!

Compassion

One garment the believer is to always wear is the garment of compassion: "clothe yourselves with compassion," writes the Apostle Paul to the Colossian Christians (Col. 3:12).

Sin makes a person hard. Living in an environment where sin is being practiced on every hand can tend to make even a Christian in-sensitive toward the needs of hurting people.

Compassion is more than the ability to *feel* with hurting people. Christian compassion responds *practically* toward the hurting and disadvantaged.

The compassion Jesus felt toward needy individuals inevitably *moved* him to *do* something for the needy.

How often we lamely excuse ourselves from becoming involved in the needs of others by reacting, "You can't help everyone." No, God doesn't call us to help everyone, but he has called us to act in love and compassion toward that one whom providence has sent our way — our "neighbor."

We can't call ourselves Christians and turn a blind eye to the needy people God has put on our doorstep: "But whoever has the world's goods, and sees his brother in need and closes his heart against him, how does the love of God abide in him?" (1 John 3:17).

You can only extend compassion according to your ability. It doesn't necessarily involve money, it may mean giving someone a ride every Sunday to church. It may mean sitting with an invalid a half-day every week. It may mean preparing and delivering a meal during a sickness. It may mean buying a new suit for your pastor. Or, it may mean taking some money God has blessed you with and giving it in his name to a needy person.

Just a few days ago, it was my privilege to sit in the presence of a compassionate Christian philanthropist. He told my wife and me that just that day he had given a thousand dollars to two people so they could pay their rent. He also related that in the past two years he had paid $350,000 in medical expenses for someone who wasn't even considered a friend. He wasn't boasting; he simply did what he believed he should.

You and I live in a day when people — even many Christian people — lack real compassion for hurting people. Let's purpose not to be one of them; instead, let us look to Jesus who time and again was moved to reach out and minister God's practical love for his hurting creatures.

Perseverance

God has called his people to steadfast faithfulness. He has marked out a course for each of us to run, and we can either run the course faithfully to the finish, or we can fail and even drop out. Life can be hard, but God is good.

As he was sitting in the open air one dreadful day in a Russian gulag, Alexsandr Solzhenitsyn (1918-2008) felt despair and gloom settling over him. This brilliant Christian writer had been sentenced to serve years in a Siberian prison by an oppressive, despotic system. He didn't know if he could survive the cruelties of this tormenting nightmare. While feeling his own pain and despair one day, a man seated next to him picked up a stick and drew the sign of the cross in the dirt. Suddenly, Solzhenitsyn gained a renewed perspective. He got up, picked up his shovel, and went back to work. Knowing that Christ, as the innocent God-man had suffered for him, his will was infused with a new energy to persevere until the end — regardless.

Just before the patriarch Jacob went to his eternal reward, he gathered all his sons around him in order to pronounce upon them his farewell blessing. Coming to Joseph, he said, "With bitterness archers attacked him; they shot at him with hostility. But his bow remained steady, his strong arms stayed limber, because of the hand of the Mighty One of Jacob, because of the Shepherd, the Rock of Israel" (Gen. 49:24). Jacob was saying that Joseph remained "steady" — persevered — in the face of extreme difficulties.

Jesus is our Model for perseverance. He faithfully followed the will of the Father for his life to the very end of his earthly sojourn. He came to help you and me to do the same.

Christ in Us

If we were exhorted by God to live out a Christlike life by depending on our own strength and ingenuity, this would be an absolute impossibility. But the good news is that our Father doesn't expect us to live like his Son without his help.

Here's the open secret of living a Christlike life: through his Holy Spirit Jesus wants to be a permanent abiding Presence in our hearts. Then, by dwelling in us, he can empower each of us to live every day to the glory of his Father and our Father: "Christ in you, the hope of glory" (Col. 1:27).

Apart from the indwelling Christ the Christian can only struggle, strive, and make endless resolutions to do better. But with the all-conquering Christ residing in us, he — with our obedient cooperation — empowers us to be grateful, humble, compassionate, persevering disciples.

On the wall to the main entrance of the Alamo in San Antonio, Texas, is a portrait with the following inscription: "James Butler Bonham (no picture of him exists). This portrait is of his nephew, Major James Bonham, deceased; who greatly resembled his uncle. It is placed here by the family that people may know the appearance of the man who died for freedom."

We have no *physical* portrait of God our Father, but he has left us a *portrait* in his Son, who is "the exact imprint of his nature" (Heb. 1:3) — so that we Christians might, through his indwelling power, model our lives after him, and become increasingly conformed to his image: "And we all, with unveiled face, beholding the glory of the Lord, are being transformed into the same image from one degree of glory to another. For this comes from the Lord who is the Spirit" (2 Cor. 3:18). May this be our fervent aspiration — to be changed increasingly into Christ's likeness.

Be encouraged, dear Christian, the Holy Spirit has been given to accomplish this very work in us. I pray the words of one of my favorite hymns, authored by Thomas Chisholm (1866-1960), will always resonate in your heart as well as mine:

> *I have one deep supreme desire,*
> *That I may be like Jesus.*
> *To this I fervently aspire,*
> *That I may be like Jesus.*
>
> *I want my heart His throne to be,*
> *So that a watching world may see*
> *His likeness shining forth in me.*
> *I want to be like Jesus.*[2]

CHAPTER 21

Why Pastors Weep

To shed tears is a natural human response to something that touches us very deeply. The degree to which people are given to tears, and the reasons for which people cry, differ as widely as the personalities involved.

Some people seem to cry at the "drop of a hat." Others never, or rarely, shed a tear. Then there are those who are so maudlin that it can be embarrassing to be in their presence sometimes; they don't appear to have any control over their emotions. On the other hand, there is a certain type of male who has been erroneously taught that to shed tears is not a masculine thing to do. Unfortunately, these men have stifled their emotions for so long that they cannot react naturally to some situations where the shedding of tears would be quite normal.

As with most things pertaining to the human condition, somewhere between these two extremes—shedding tears for apparently no reason, and the inability to shed tears for any reason—we find an emotionally stable and psychologically healthy individual.

Tear ducts are one of the evidences of our being fearfully and wonderfully made by our Creator-God. God made us with the capacity to shed tears. From the wails of a newborn baby entering the world to the shedding of tears at a grave—to weep is part of our human condition.

The reasons for which we cry are vast. A little girl hugging her returned lost puppy cries. A father, looking on as his son receives an achievement award, sheds a tear. A mother weeps for joy when the nurse places her newborn child on her breast. A student cries upon discovering he has failed his final exam. Tears are part-and-parcel of who we are as human beings.

Sprinkled throughout our holy Scriptures are accounts of a variety of individuals who shed tears for the right reasons (one can shed tears for the wrong reasons: e.g., not getting our selfish way). For example, there was the prophet Jeremiah who wept over the sins of God's people so often that today we call him "The Weeping Prophet." There was Hannah, who wanted a child so badly that she wept in the presence of Eli the priest. There was David, who frequently wept, as we know so well from reading the Psalms. There was the Apostle Paul who wrote about how often he shed tears as he remembered his converts in his prayers. But most movingly of all, there was the Lord Jesus: "As he approached Jerusalem and saw the city, he wept over it" (Luke 19:4 NIV). How can we not be *moved* when reading such an account?

Then, there was Timothy, the overseer of the Ephesian Church. Writing to him from a Roman prison, the Apostle Paul, his spiritual mentor and intimate friend, writes, "I constantly remember you in my prayers night and day, longing to see you, even as I recall your tears" (2 Tim. 1:4 NASB). It could very well be that what Paul has reference to here was the occasion when he left for Macedonia, leaving Timothy behind. Possibly Timothy was so overcome with emotion at Paul's departure, that he wept, though we cannot be certain of the interpretation.

While this may be a possible interpretation of the passage, I see another possibility. Inasmuch as Timothy had the responsibility of overseeing the Church of Ephesus, could it be that he was shedding tears for reasons other than Paul's departure? I think so. And many pastors would agree; for faithful pastors know what it means to weep—and weep frequently, if not actual tears, at least in their hearts.

With this in mind, let's ask ourselves, Why is it that pastors weep? What does Christ's faithful pastor experience in the depths of his soul that causes him to occasionally break out in tears? Let's examine a few possibilities.

Pastors Weep Because They Care

Hired hands don't weep—because they're hired hands. Shepherds weep—because they're true shepherds, because they care.

A surgeon who performs surgeries day after day, and often several in the same day, has developed a professional *detachment* from his patients. He protects himself against getting too emotionally involved. After all, the reasoning goes, the human psyche can only absorb so much trauma.

But with the pastor it is different. It is different because eternal verities and souls are involved. Real people with real needs require a *feeling* shepherd as their spiritual overseer. The caring pastor knows what it is to weep with those who weep. He sits where his people sit and feels their sins and their grief and their disappointments and their regrets and their sorrows. A cold, detached professional may be expert in shuffling papers and meeting deadlines and achieving goals. But only a *caring* pastor feels deeply enough for his people to weep with them and over them. One doesn't shed tears for those he has no concern for. A pastor with a shepherd's heart will weep *for* his people and *with* his people because he genuinely cares for them.

Pastors Weep for the Unconverted

How can a pastor be considered a man of God if he doesn't care deeply enough for the lost to shed tears over them? If we believe what we say we believe about the eternal destinies of those without a saving knowledge of Jesus Christ, how can we not be moved to tears? Or have we changed and reconsidered the doctrine of eternal punishment? Possibly we have unwittingly fallen prey to the insidious doctrine of universalism. Maybe we don't believe some people are actually going to a place called Hell. If that is our belief, then it is no wonder that we don't weep over the lost.

No, thank God, there are thousands of faithful evangelical pastors who believe that apart from trusting in the Lord Jesus Christ one cannot be saved, and they weep over those they earnestly desire to come to Christ.

Rescue the perishing, care for the dying;
Snatch them in pity from sin and the grave;
Weep o'er the erring one, lift up the fallen,
Tell them of Jesus, the Mighty to save.[1]

Pastors Weep Over Deceived People

A true shepherd doesn't take the salvation of his people for granted. He realizes that merely because a person has been a church member for forty years, or on the church board for twenty years, or sat in a church pew most of his life, that having such credentials doesn't equal eternal life.

This pastor is knowledgeable enough in the things of God to know that some of his people are trusting in their baptism or communion observance, church membership and good works, instead of trusting in the Lord Jesus Christ for his and her salvation. He can't be angry with these self-deceived parishioners if he truly cares for them. No, their blind condition will move him to tears – if not in his pulpit ministry, then in his private intercessions.

When he looks out over his congregation from Sunday to Sunday, this pastor views some of the older members who show no evidence of the life of God in their hearts. (Yes, pastors can often tell.) And it breaks his shepherd's heart. He doesn't rant and rave at them. He doesn't scold them week after week; before he received a shepherd's heart he used to scold. But he learned from the Great Shepherd that "the anger does not achieve the righteousness of God" (James 1:20). The pastor preaches the Word of God faithfully and lovingly, with a tear-filled heart, hoping their eyes will be opened. He lives with an ever-present ache in his heart for such people.

Pastors Weep Over Careless People

It is a sad but true church reality – many Christians are living careless lives; and one of the greatest burdens – if not *the* greatest – the caring pastor carries is the constant weight he feels over his careless sheep.

This carelessness manifests itself in a multitude of ways. With many, they are living with confused priorities. Dwelling as we are in an age that increasingly resembles Sodom, the pressures of our godless culture tend to shape the lifestyles of many of our churchgoers more than does the Holy Spirit. Since the average Christian has little experiential knowledge of the indwelling fullness of the Holy Spirit, and knows almost nothing about an intense hunger and thirst for God and his righteousness, I suppose we shouldn't be surprised at the low level of spiritual maturity filling our pews.

If one hasn't made a full surrender to the lordship of Jesus Christ, and is not being transformed and renewed in his and her mind daily, it's no wonder that one's priorities are confused. Clearly, such people will have a greater appetite for pleasure than they will for God and the things of God. To pursue a self-centered lifestyle is natural for them since they are not living a life in the Spirit.

But it breaks many a pastor's heart. When the pastor sees leaders and members missing a prayer meeting or a church service because of confused, worldly priorities—it is cause for weeping. Even though this pastor fully realizes that this is one of the signs of the end time, nevertheless, he can never rest comfortably knowing some of his sheep love the world more than they love Christ.

Pastors Weep with the Weeping

I'll never forget my first experience of weeping with those who weep. I was a young pastor, and one our mothers had given birth to a beautiful girl. The physician informed the parents that because of a serious congenital defect the child would not live long.

The entire church family took the matter to the Lord. Although I confided in no one, I believed that the child would live. When I received the devastating news at 2:00 o'clock one morning that the child had died, I was stunned. I dressed quickly and hurried over to the home where the parents and grandparents had gathered. When I entered the living room, I was struggling to control myself. I wept.

I found out later that though none of the family remembered any of the words of consolation I had offered that dark night, they remembered my tears. And the tears formed a lasting bond.

There is so much in our culture that contributes to the desensitization of our humanity. As pastors, we must guard ourselves against becoming insensitive to the needs of our people. It's true, there are times when a disorderly sheep needs "shearing." But let's not take it out on all the sheep — week after week!

As lay people, let's make sure that we don't bring grief to the heart of our shepherd and spiritual overseer. May your pastor be able to say of you that you are a joy to pastor and not a burden. If he sheds tears over you, may it not be because of your carelessness and indifference.

Pastors Weep for *Joy.*

Just as there is rejoicing among the angels in Heaven when a sinner comes home to God, a caring pastor often weeps for joy when he sees people come to Christ, as well as observing marked growth among his converts. Tears of sorrow that were shed over a person's lost estate are turned into tears of gratitude when the lost have been found and the blind receive their sight. Again and again, it has been my privilege through the years to shed tears of joy when seeing a lost sheep return to the fold, or watching a prodigal return to his Father.

Pastors Weep Over Their Own *Shortcomings*

A pastor differs from his people only in his calling. Though a faithful pastor is deserving of great respect, he, nonetheless, is made of the same "stuff" as his parishioners. Since this is true, pastors also battle with emotional highs and lows, with discouragements and disappointments, and with failures to always be a wise man of God in every situation.

I'm not talking about moral failures of the grossest kind — such men do not belong in the ministry. But in every pastor's own spiritual pilgrimage — if he's honest — there will be times when he will shed tears because he was not as gentle and kind as he should have been, not as patient and considerate as he could have been, not as caring and courageous as a situation warranted, or not as careful in practicing moral discrimination as he ought. Thus he weeps, and when necessary, confesses his failures and sins to God, and apologizes to others when necessary.

As the man of God grows in grace and maturity, as he learns to abide in Christ and walk among his people in all humility, he will shed fewer tears because of his own lack. However, knowing himself better than anyone else, he never reaches a level of grace where he no longer has any debts to confess.

The godly pastor lives with a constant groan in his heart because he craves more and more of God's holiness; he intensely desires more of the mind of Christ; he wants to be more like Jesus. Such a pastor fully realizes that apart from Christ he is nothing and can do nothing. He has an insatiable appetite for God. This in itself is cause for plenty of tears as pours out his heart to God on his knees.

Pastors Weep Because They Want to Be More Fruitful

The late English evangelist Leonard Ravenhill (1907-1994) recalled a striking encounter he had one day.

I remember going down High Holborne in London a few years ago. . . . A little lady was going to the mail box. There she was, very, very stooped and she shakily put her mail into the box; then she turned to go into a building. Somebody asked me, "Do you know who that is?" And I said, "Not the slightest idea." "That is the widow of Hugh Price Hughes." At one time the king of the Methodist pulpit in England. His daughter gave us a huge biography of her father. And she said, "When he came back on a Sunday night from the service, if no one had been saved, he would be inconsolable. You couldn't comfort him. He wouldn't eat, he wouldn't drink. He wouldn't even take his long coat off. He threw himself over his bed and he sobbed and he sobbed and he sobbed and said, 'Why? Why? Why?'"[2]

While actual tears may not come easily for many people, including pastors, yet whether one sheds physical tears or not, at least we should all have a weeping heart — especially shepherds of sheep. Pastors are in good company whenever they weep — after all, the prophets of old, the holy apostles, and the Lord Jesus Christ often shed tears.

Give me tears, O Lord — tears for the lost, tears for Your disobedient children, tears for the growth of Your church, tears over needy leaders, tears for my own failures, tears of joy and gratitude for Your great salvation.

CHAPTER 22

Power and Authority in the Church

I have spent practically my entire life in the church. From just a few days old when my dear godly mother carried me to my first church service, to over fifty years of ministry in the service of my Lord, the church has been my native environment.

The church has been the love of my life. The communion of the saints, the prayers and songs ascending in thanksgiving, praise and worship, the sermons preached with both passion and power — all this and much more, have been used by its Architect and Builder to make me the person I am, warts and all.

I have given my life to Christ in the service of the church. I have no regrets; I would do it all over again — only hopefully much better. I am not cynical, bitter nor disillusioned; but neither am I naive or blind.

As one of the church's most unworthy and fallible members, I must say with a burden of love: the Lord of the Church stands on the outside of many of his churches, wishing to be invited in. And does not this coincide with John's vision of Christ on the island of Patmos? "Behold, I stand at the door and knock" (Rev. 3:20 NASB).

Having had a wide variety of ecclesiastical experiences, I am convinced that the average church janitor, organist and donor exercises more power and control in the church than does the Head of the church, the Lord Jesus Christ.

Prior to his ascension to the Father's right hand, the risen, triumphant Savior announced to the Eleven Apostles: "All authority in heaven and on earth has been given to me" (Matt. 28:18 NIV). Authority is always delegated; power and control are self-assumed, man-dominated. One comes from above, the other from beneath. Jesus never spoke nor acted on his own initiative: "Behold, I have come . . . to do your will, O God." "The words that I say to you I do not speak on My own initiative, but the Father abiding in Me does His works" (Heb. 10:7; John 14:10 NASB).

Christ as the Savior and Head of the church and the Holy Spirit as its indwelling Presence, have been specially authorized by God the Father to provide the church with oversight and direction through its earthly representatives: apostles, prophets, evangelists, pastors and teachers, elders and deacons (see Eph. 4:11; 1 Tim. 3:1-13).

To provide it with a clear, objective guide, the church has been given a God-breathed document—the written Word of God—as the authoritative manual for its life, conduct, mission and administration (see 2 Tim. 3:16). Sadly, in our own day, too often we see the church cut off from its Head. Human traditions, local customs and self-appointed leaders have more power in a local congregation than does Christ and the written Word of God.

One of God's prophetic voices in the twentieth century saw this problem far more clearly than I. Just a short time prior to his death in 1963, A. W. Tozer (1897-1963) wrote an article titled *The Waning Authority of Christ in the Churches.*

> The Lordship of Jesus Christ is not quite forgotten among Christians, but it has been relegated to the hymnal where all responsibility toward it may be comfortably discharged in a glow of religious emotion. Or if it is taught as a theory in the classroom it is rarely applied to practical living. The idea that the Man Christ Jesus has absolute final authority over the whole church and over its members in every detail of their lives is simply not now accepted as true by the rank and file of evangelical Christians.
>
> What we do is this: We accept the Christianity of our group as being identical with that of Christ and his apostles. The beliefs, the practices, the ethics, the activities of our group are equated with the Christianity of the New Testa-

ment. Whatever our group thinks or says or does is scriptural, no questions asked. It is assumed that all our Lord expects of us is that we busy ourselves with the activities of the group. In doing so we are keeping the commandments of Christ. . . .

What church board consults our Lord's words to decide matters under discussion? Let anyone reading this who has had experience on a church board try to recall the times or time when any board member read from the Scriptures to make a point, or when any chairman suggested that the brethren should see what instructions the Lord had for them on a particular question. Board meetings are habitually opened with a formal prayer or a "season of prayer"; after that the Head of the Church is respectfully silent while the real rulers take over. . . .

What Christian when faced with a moral problem goes straight to the Sermon on the Mount or other New Testament Scripture for the authoritative answer? Who lets the words of Christ be final on giving, . . . the bringing up of a family, personal habits, tithing, entertainment, buying, selling and other important matters? . . . .

For the true Christian the one supreme test for the present soundness and ultimate worth of everything religious must be the place our Lord occupies in it. Is he Lord or symbol? Is he in charge of the project or merely one of the crew? Does he decide things or only help to carry out the plan of others? All religious activities, from the simplest act of an individual Christian to the ponderous and expensive operations of a whole denomination, may be proved by the answer to the question. *Is Jesus Christ Lord in this act?* Whether our works prove to be wood, hay and stubble or gold and silver and precious stones in that great day will depend upon the right answer to that question.[1]

We need to seriously consider what steps serious-minded Christians and church leaders can take in order to honor Christ's authority and lordship in the church? Permit me to suggest the following.

Every church leader (elders and deacons) must live in total submission to Jesus Christ, the Head of the church. If the leaders aren't living in an authentic vital relationship to Christ as they should, then they should repent and get thoroughly right with God. If they fail to repent, then they should do the honorable thing — resign their position. There are far too many backslidden, worldly-minded, and self-centered leaders who are preventing the church from moving forward as God expects it to. They love the praise of men, cater to wealthy and prominent members, explain away the Word of God, lack a passion for Christ, and are sinning in their personal life. They are a plague in the body of Christ. Christ expects the church to be led by Spirit-filled, God-honoring, godly leaders. This is basic.

1 Timothy 3:1-13 is God's standard for every church leader. And we need to do more than just pay lip service to this text. These qualifications cannot be viewed as options or simply a stated *ideal*. Four times Paul uses the word "must." And remember, these qualifications were first laid down for leaders in the first-century church for men who had come to Christ from a pagan culture.

In our unsanctified desire to be all things to all people in order that we might please everyone, we have forsaken the biblical basics. The power of wealth, friendships, family relationships, the fear of saying *No* to anyone, and a host of other rationalizations, have paralyzed our ability to stand for anything. If our leaders don't measure up to the minimum stated qualifications in 1 Timothy 3:1-13, they are disqualified for leadership.

How might we in an observable way recognize the authority of Christ in our churches?

When leaders meet together to conduct the business of the church, consulting the Lord by means of prayer and Scripture ought to be the norm. A perfunctory opening prayer to a business meeting is an insult to the Head of the church. The very essence of prayer is dependence. When we fail to take the authority of Christ seriously we don't feel the need to consult him.

In a recent conversation with a Christian businessman, he told me the leaders in his church had been conducting a series of meetings with a view to expanding the church's outreach and ministry. He said they were waiting upon God for clear direction. In his words: "This time we're not going to ask God to bless *our* plans; instead, we're waiting for his plans, then we know what we do will have God's blessing." Wise leaders!

Where are there any business meetings any more where church leaders actually get down on their *knees* to pray? Have we become so proud and self-assured that we can't bow before the Lord in a posture of humility and dependence? May God have mercy on us! We are in such a rush to get to the *important* things: our agenda, our proposals, our ideas, and our suggestions — that we have no time for Christ. Do I hear him knocking from the *outside* trying to get our attention?

Rigid regularity should never be allowed to quench Spirit-spontaneity. Structures, as essential as they are, must never be allowed to quench spontaneous, sovereign moves of the Spirit. Our agendas and orders of service should be developed with a conscious realization that we are always open to the Lord of the church to change anything we have planned.

Consider: the Book of Acts would never have been written as it was if the apostles and the Early Church saints had stifled the spontaneous moves of the Spirit. If the apostles had insisted on their pre-planned agendas, there would never have been the outpouring of the Spirit on the day of Pentecost, healings would never have occurred, doors of outreach and expanded missions would have been stifled, and fresh infillings of the Spirit would never have been experienced. The church would have been a sterile, well-structured religious institution, attractive to one's esthetical senses possibly, but fruitless and powerless.

One cannot be a student of the Bible without noticing that our God is a God of design and order. But neither can one read the Scriptures without being struck by the fact that the same God who designed what we call natural and spiritual laws is the same God who periodically invades his creation and church in order to move in a sovereign spontaneous way. Blessed are the leaders who know this and minister accordingly.

Christ has not authorized anyone to dominate his church. Depending on the personality and culture of the leader, some leaders may insist on their proposals being accepted by the group in a crude and aggressive manner, while other personalities may be more subtle in asserting their will over others. Either way, the "ark of God" often stalls because a dominant, self-willed leader insists on having it his way or no way.

This was Diotrephes' problem — he insisted on having his own way. Hear what the Apostle John had to say about him: "I wrote to the church, but Diotrephes, who loves to be first, will have nothing to do with us" (3 John 9 NIV). Pride rejects God-appointed leadership because it loves to assert itself, it wants to control others.

Realizing leaders would be subject to great temptation in this matter of administering God's work with humility, the Apostle Peter exhorts the leaders of his day to exercise their ministry without "domineering" the members of Christ's body (see 1 Pet. 5:3 ESV). If the Lordship of Jesus Christ is to be honored in his churches, then the humility of Christ must characterize its leaders. Pride insists on having its own way; humility is willing to recognize the wisdom and will of God coming through another brother: "But the wisdom from above is first pure, then peaceable, gentle, open to reason [willing to yield], full of mercy and good fruits, impartial and sincere" (James 3:17 ESV).

What about it, my friend, is Jesus Christ the ruling authority in your own life and the life of your church? Or is the Lord of the church knocking at your door or the door of your church seeking admission in order to be your Administrator? Is your church being controlled by self-willed, worldly leaders, who push their own selfish agendas and programs, or by Spirit-filled, humble men who consciously seek the will and wisdom of God in every meeting?

In his Introduction to 2 Corinthians in *The Message*, Eugene Peterson wisely remarks how the Apostle Paul handled his leadership role among the churches.

> Because leadership is necessarily an exercise of authority, it easily shifts into an exercise of power. But the minute it does that, it begins to inflict damage on both the leader and the led. Paul, studying Jesus, had learned a kind of leadership in which he managed to stay out of the way so that others could

deal with God without having to go through him. All who are called to exercise leadership in whatever capacity — parent or coach, pastor or president, teacher or manager — can be grateful to Paul for this letter, and to the Corinthians for provoking it.[2]

The church is in need of faithful under-shepherds of Christ's flock — not hirelings and charlatans, not self-promoters and ladder-climbers, not self-centered agenda-driven CEOs, but true God-called, Spirit-led men, who will serve the flock with humility and gentleness.

Would you now join with me in praying this prayer?

O Christ, you are Lord, you are my Lord. I love to be controlled by You. Enable me to practice your humility in every church setting. Help me to be conscious of your sovereign Lordship each time we gather in your name. Help me not to want to lead others as much as I want to be led by You. Be pleased to give our church godly, Spirit-anointed, Spirit-led,, Spirit-controlled leaders. Amen.

CHAPTER 23

To God Be the Glory

O ne inescapable sign discernibly marks all of our Lord's closest followers: they consciously endeavor to give our Majestic God all the glory all the time in all things.

To give God glory is to speak the language of angels, patriarchs, prophets, apostles and saints. Angels at the birth of Christ exclaimed: "Glory to God in the highest" (Luke 2:14).[1] Following Achan's sin, Joshua exhorted Achan: "My son, give glory to the LORD, the God of Israel, and give him the praise" (Josh. 7:10). Israel's sweet psalmist urged the congregation: "Ascribe to the LORD, O mighty ones, ascribe to the LORD glory and strength" (Psa. 29:1). The opening words of Mary's Magnificat reads, "My soul glorifies the Lord" (Luke 1:46). Ephesians 3:21 is typical of the Apostle Paul's recognition of the One deserving all glory: "unto him be glory in the church." Within the context of these Scriptures, the term glory is understood to mean "praise" and "credit,"; "to give that which is due."

To give God glory is to acknowledge God as the primary cause and the fundamental source of every good. His creatures are to ascribe to him glory because of his creative and redemptive activities: "You are worthy, our Lord and God to receive glory and honor and power, for you created all things, and by your will they were created and have their being" (Rev. 4:11). "Worthy is the Lamb who was slain, to receive power and wealth and wisdom and honor and glory and praise!" (Rev. 5:12).

We are to glorify God because he, and he alone is worthy to receive the glory. And yet, how we fallen, ego-driven Christians maneuver to shine the spotlight of glory and praise upon ourselves instead of deflecting it all to the Worthy One.

I recently listened in amazement to a pastor advertise one of his recorded sermon series by saying, "Undoubtedly, these are the greatest sermons ever preached from this pulpit!" I had to ask myself: *Is he the only one who ever preached from that pulpit; and if he was, where is the humility in such a remark?*

Sometime ago I received an e-mail request from a brother in Texas who is a relatively new convert. He introduced himself as an "up and coming evangelist, who has something to say to this generation." A few days ago I read an advertisement for a Christian concert artist "who has one of the finest voices" among Christian singers.

Pride invariably makes comparisons, and when it surfaces in the church it compares itself with other preachers and pastors, and other voices and singers. Thus, even in the church we commonly hear the language of "greatest," "best," "finest," "biggest," "highest," "more successful," etc. Does this sound all too familiar?

Lamentably, the marketplace has entered the church. The language of the world has become the language of the church, because the church has failed to give God the glory. We pay lip service to the Lord while slyly (and most times not so slyly) taking the credit ourselves.

Jesus saw this defect among some of his own followers. Following a successful evangelism campaign, his disciples reported: "Lord, even the demons submit to us in your name." Our Lord instinctively heard the misplaced emphasis—the "us" was more pronounced than "in your name." Jesus responded, "I saw lightning fall from heaven . . . do not rejoice that the spirits submit to you, but rejoice that your names are written in heaven" (see Luke 10:17-20).

What did Jesus mean by his response? As followers of Christ, we should never glory in anything the Lord has accomplished through us. Instead, we should give glory to God for what *he* has done for us, remembering that it was a failure to give God all the glory which proved to be the downfall of an angel--and a sudden fall it was!

There's a little legend which illustrates this matter of how we tend to accept the praise and the glory instead of passing it along to the Lord. The story goes like this: On Palm Sunday, when the Lord entered Jerusalem riding on a donkey, he was received with shouts of "Hosanna to the Son of David" (of course, this part of the story is true). That evening the donkey told his fellow donkeys in the stable: "If you could have seen how they glorified me in Jerusalem today! They called me 'son of David.' I had never known before the name of the donkey who was my father. I was very pleased to find out he was called David. And, furthermore, the crowd seemed very determined to make me king. They threw their clothes before me on the road in order that I might walk in softness. I suppose they will come tomorrow to enthrone me. I imagine that when a donkey becomes king, he gets plenty of hay and is not made to carry burdens any longer!" What a dumb donkey! He didn't realize the glory belonged to his Rider.

Paul prayed, "unto him be glory in the church." Of all people, the people of God should be the people from whom God is receiving the highest glory. In "the church" — the redeemed, the saved, the justified, the sanctified.

Prophets, apostles, evangelists, pastors, musicians, church leaders-none of these are to receive that which is due to God alone. They are not to receive it because they don't deserve it. Only God deserves the glory. Human organizations don't deserve the glory. How we love to brag about our ministry, denomination and local church. How we exult in our theologies, institutions and histories. Walking into some churches one is struck by brass plates conspicuously located on walls and furniture. Can't we give anything to the Lord without insisting our name be on it? Must pastors and church committees appeal to human vanity in order to raise sufficient funds? And then we have the audacity to say we gave it to the glory of God? Whatever happened to giving without the left hand knowing what the right hand has done? (see Matt. 6:3-4).

Could the reality be that there is so much self-exaltation in the church because we have forgotten who we are: redeemed sinners who have been delivered from the wrath to come; that we are nothing but unprofitable and unworthy servants of a gracious and merciful God? The language of our soul should ever be that of the publican with bowed head in the temple: "God, have mercy on me, a sinner!" (Luke 18:13). Could it be that we are to self-absorbed to give God all the glory? Could it be that our egos are so fragile, unsanctified, proud, that we are so preoccupied with what we think we have accomplished, that we fail to see the Holy One who indeed is worthy to receive all the glory?

Can God trust you to give him all the glory? When the late Methodist evangelist John R. Church was a young and aspiring preacher, he was invited to give the commencement address at Asbury College in the 1930s. Later in recounting that event with Dr. Dennis F. Kinlaw, Church related the following account.

> "The place was packed. Excitement was high. God was with me and I soared. I thought, *I have this audience in the palm of my hand. I can do anything I want with them.* Suddenly, a cold chill moved over me. I closed the service immediately, went to my room, and got on my knees. I said, 'God, if you'll forgive me, I'll never be guilty of that again.'
>
> "For years afterward, I met people who said, 'Dr. Church, do you remember when you were at Asbury for commencement?' It happened so many times that I knew what was coming. They would say, 'You know, I have never heard such oratory.'
>
> "I would ask, 'What did I preach about?'
>
> "I never met a person who could recall the text or the topic I had preached about," Dr. Church said. "All they remembered was the oratory."[2]

Isn't it time for Christians to repent—to repent for *angling* for some of the glory? Are some of us guilty of promoting ourselves instead of Christ? Preaching ourselves instead of Christ? Exalting our ministries, programs and successes instead of glorifying Christ? Who are we talking about? Who are we praising? Who's getting the credit? Who's wanting the credit? Isn't it time for us to humble ourselves before the Lord of the flaming eyes and the two-edged sword?

Let each of us present ourselves to the Refiner of hearts anew, allowing him to purify us afresh, that we may always give God the glory that belongs to him alone.

Knowing that the deadly sin of pride would prove to be his downfall, unless avoided, when George Whitefield (1714-1770) was preparing to be ordained as an Anglican minister, he prayed the following prayer: "Dearest Redeemer, make me humble, prepare me for Thy future mercies; and whenever Thou seest me in danger of being exalted above measure, graciously send a thorn in the flesh, so that Thy blessings may not prove to be my ruin."[3] When Johann Sebastian Bach began writing a new composition, he would write, "*Jesu Juva*" (Jesus, help). When finished, he would write, "*Soli Deo Gloria*" (to God alone be the glory).[4]

I couldn't say it any better.

A final note: We need to remember this truth in our worship services. We are giving glory to God if we applaud *Him* following songs of praise and worship; we are giving glory to the musicians if we applaud *them* following their songs of praise and worship. The one response from the congregants is an act of worship; the other response has transposed worship into a performance. The one response, exalts God; the other response, exalts man.

For the Christian, let all the glory be given to God alone.

To You, and to You alone, O Lord,
   be all the glory, praise and highest honor.
Forgive us for taking to ourselves
   what belongs to Your name now and forever.

CHAPTER 24

Living to the Glory of God

The formulators of the *Westminster Confession of Faith* got it right when they affirmed, "The chief end of man is to glorify God and to enjoy him forever." To live to the glory of God is the reason for our very existence as well as our highest calling.

In the Greek language, in which the New Testament was written, the word for "man" (*anthropos*) literally means the "upper-looking one." Even the pagan Greek wordsmiths — when the language was being developed — realized that man existed for something (Someone?) beyond and outside of themselves. We, who have received a more perfect revelation of God through his written and living Word than they, know *Who* we are to look up to. Man was created and redeemed by God to look up to and worship and glorify the God and Father of the Lord Jesus Christ, the only true and living God.

Whenever man forgets *why* he is on this planet, or fails to pursue a life that glorifies God, he becomes the saddest of all God's creatures. Conversely, whenever men and women live solely to the glory of God, they enjoy an inner sense of wellbeing and peace and an outer poise as they walk through a fallen, disintegrating world, fulfilling their God-called destinies.

The Scriptures are replete with tragic examples of those who failed to live to the glory of God; they also provide us with beautiful narratives of many who were totally centered on bringing honor and

praise to their Creator-Redeemer. There are also some striking illustrations in the Word of God of those who characteristically lived their
lives to God's glory, but either because of pride and stubbornness, or
a moment of fleshly weakness, or an unwillingness to surrender fully
to God's sovereign claim upon their lives, they failed to live for God's
glory and resorted to self-glory.

Biblical Pointers

Because the Bible has so much to say about giving glory, honor,
and praise to God, it behooves every sincere and earnest disciple of
the Lord Jesus Christ to cultivate a lifestyle of living to God's glory.
From Genesis to Revelation, God exhorts mankind through his
prophets, poets, priests and apostles, to both *give* glory to and *live* to
God's glory. Giving glory to God is an act of worship; *living* to the
glory of God is also worship. The one may be a spontaneous expression of a moment; the other is a learned habit, flowing from the man
and woman who know their place before "the High and Lofty One
Who inhabits eternity, whose name is Holy" (Isa. 57:15 NKJV).

The most comprehensive and moving expressions of creatures
giving glory to God are shown to us in the Revelation given to the
Apostle John on Patmos Island. If only reads the last book of the New
Testament trying to figure out the chronology of end time events, he
will miss out on something far more important. But if one meditates
on the songs in the Book of Revelation, as one should read and sing
from a hymnal, then he will discover some of the most exalted and
inspired hymns ever penned. For it's in that book where we hear the
voices of mysterious living creatures, angelic beings, and the church
caught up repeatedly in rapturous praise to the Worthy One. Unfall-
en heavenly creatures know how to give glory to God.

". . . to Him be the glory and the dominion for ever and ever.
Amen" (1:6).[1]

"Worthy are you, our Lord and our God, to receive glory and
honor and power; for you created all things, and because of
Your will they existed, and were created" (4:11).

"Worthy is the Lamb that was slain to receive power and riches and wisdom and might and honor and glory and blessing" (5:12).

"To Him who sits on the throne, and to the Lamb, be blessing and honor and glory and dominion for ever and ever" (5:13).

"In that hour there was a great earthquake, and a tenth of the city fell; seven thousand people were killed in the earthquake, and the rest were terrified and gave glory to the God of heaven" (11:13).

". . . and he said with a loud voice, 'Fear God, and give Him glory, because the hour of His judgment has come'" (14:7).

What were these creatures doing when they gave glory and honor to God? What is God telling his people to do when he says that we should direct glory and honor to him? Simply this: As both an act of worship and a life to be lived, to give glory and honor to God means to give God the *reverence, respect* and *credit* due him for all he has done for us as the Creator of all things and as the Redeemer of humankind.

The four living creatures, twenty-four elders, myriads of angels, every created thing in Heaven and earth, as depicted in the Revelation, give glory and honor to God for both God's creative and redemptive activities on behalf of mankind. The fact is, all of God's creation, except for fallen man, are endlessly acknowledging the worthiness of God both day and night: "they do not cease to say, 'Holy, Holy, Holy is the Lord God, the Almighty, who was and who is and who is to come'" (Rev. 4:8).

If the Lord's will should "be done on earth as it is in heaven" (Matt. 6:10), we can become a part of the answer to that petition by daily living to the glory of God. How might we do so? Reader, how can you and I—as profound and humbling as the thought is—live to God's glory? How might we fulfill our noble calling in this life, living each and every day to the glory of our worthy God and Father of the Lord Jesus Christ? Let's consider together some of the following ways that we can live to bring glory to God.

A Worshiping Tongue

Did you notice how the *tongue* was employed in worshipful praise by all the singing creatures in the Revelation? The same way it has been for all of God's worshiping saints from the beginning of time down through this present age. From the instinctive response of the newborn, forgiven child of God looking up into the face of his heavenly Father, to the aged, weather-worn saint worshiping on her face before the Throne — giving glory and honor to God is as natural to the soul as it is for a mother to pass along her milk to a nursing child. Each was made for the other.

I was reading recently the conversion story of the Church of the Nazarene evangelist Bud Robinson (1860-1942). After leaving a West Texas Methodist camp meeting altar, where he experienced God's saving grace, Bud recounts: "The Lord marched out all the stars of heaven on a dress parade for my special benefit, and the stars leaped and hopped and skipped and jumped and turned somersaults and clapped their hands and laughed all night. The Lord showed me that it was all at his expense and did not cost me one nickel. I just lay [down] and laughed all night."

Having spent the night following his conversion sleeping under an ox wagon (he was poor and the times were primitive), Bud writes,

The next morning, as day was beginning to break, I crawled from under the ox wagon and went out on the camp ground. I watched the sun rise in all its grandeur and glory. The whole heavens were lighted up. I would look in one direction and it would appear to be like mountains of oranges; in another direction, like tons of strawberries and I'd look in another direction and it was like tons of ice cream. It seemed to me that the angels were having strawberries and ice cream for breakfast. I turned and looked at a great flock of clouds in another direction and it had the appearance of a great flock of sheep with their wool on fire. Just about that time heaven came down to the earth and I was so blest that soon I was leaping up and down, clapping my hands and praising God as loud as I could shout."[2]

Of course, we know that the heavens always declare the glory of

God, but newly converted Bud Robinson had only had his eyes recently opened to it and was giving God glory along with the heavens.

Then we have a beautiful testimony and example of a godly person like hymn writer Frances Havergal (1836-1879), who lived her entire life to God's glory. Her remarkable usefulness began when she consecrated herself fully to the Lord Jesus Christ. Her complete devotion was strikingly expressed by her own hand:

> *Take my will, and make it Thine; it shall be no longer mine.*
> *Take my heart, it is Thine own; it shall be Thy royal throne.*
> *Take my love, my Lord, I pour at Thy feet its treasure store.*
> *Take myself, and I will be ever, only, all for Thee.*[3]

One of her dying whispers was, "I did so want to glorify Him in every step of my way."[4]

Whether at the beginning of one's conversion to the Lord Jesus Christ, as in the case of Bud Robinson, or in one's dying breath, as was the case of Frances Havergal, we were all made by creation and redemption to give glory to God with our words and with our life.

In Jesus' Name

Although the passage is found within the context of how corporate worship is to be conducted in a local church, the principle is applicable to all of life: "Whatever you do in word or deed, do all in the name of the Lord Jesus, giving thanks through him to God the Father" (Col. 3:17). To act and speak in Jesus' name is to acknowledge the lordship of Jesus Christ in whatever we say and do. It is to live out even the so-called mundane tasks of life—eating and drinking—"to the glory of God" (see 1 Cor. 10:31).

That brings to mind a pungent truth from the pen of A. W. Tozer (1897-1963): "It is not what a man does that determines whether his work is sacred or secular; it is *why* he does it. The motive is everything. Let a man sanctity the Lord God in his heart and he can thereafter do no common act. All he does is good and acceptable to God through Jesus Christ. For such a man, living itself will be sacramental and the whole world a sanctuary."[5]

Recently one evening my wife Emily and I were parked at a local

Dairy Queen eating our ice cream cones. Softly in the background, one of our instrumental CD hymns was playing "Just As I Am." While we both were enjoying this sacred music, I said, "You know, Charlotte Elliott had no idea when she penned those words the extent to which God would use them." Then, after Emily and I thought about that for a moment, we both agreed that God's Word affirms that any and everything done or said in Jesus' name has a lasting quality to it—it will never die. It will never die because it was done to the glory of God.

Our Bodies as Holy Temples

When the inspired apostle reminded the immature Thessalonian believers, "For this is the will of God, your sanctification" (1 Thess. 4:3), he did so within the context of addressing the subject of sexual behavior. Some of these converts had fallen into sinful conduct following their confession of faith, or had never broken their sinful lifestyle. God says to such through the pen of the inspired writer: "abstain from sexual immorality. . . . For God has not called us for the purpose of impurity but in sanctification" (see 1 Thess. 4:1-8).

In his first letter to the Corinthian Church, Paul exhorts these Christians to "Flee immorality" (1 Cor. 6:18). Why? Because "your body is the temple of the Holy Spirit who is in you. . . . For you have been bought with a price: therefore glorify God in your body."

Just as we should never desecrate an earthly sanctuary that has been consecrated to God for sacred purposes, so the Christian is called by God to cleanse his consecrated temple—the body—"from all defilement of the flesh and spirit, perfecting holiness in the fear of God" (2 Cor. 7:1).

The Christian who takes a flippant attitude about what he eats and drinks (including the portions), what he views—everything he does with his body—and merely shrugs his shoulders and says, "It isn't anyone's business!"—is saying in effect that it isn't God's "business" either. God is certainly concerned about the Christian's reputation in the world and his influence in church, but he is equally concerned with how we treat our bodies. Thus we are called by God to "present [our] bodies a living and holy sacrifice, acceptable to God, which is [our] spiritual service of worship" (Rom 12:1).

Since our bodies are to be consecrated vessels, we are to glorify God in how we treat them and how we use them. Therefore, we are not to indulge our bodies in sinful practices — such as sexual immorality. Instead, it brings glory to God when our bodies are vehicles through which the Spirit's fruit can grow in balanced maturity (see Gal. 5:22-23).

Is Jesus Lord?

There is one thing as Christians we cannot do simultaneously: give glory to God while glorifying ourselves. We must do one or the other. He will not share his glory with another. To paraphrase the words of Moses: "Oh, I wish that all of the Lord's people were God-glorifiers!" (Num. 11:29). Oh, that every pastor and evangelist, every elder and deacon, every musician and worship leader, every parishioner — including you and me — would worship and serve, act and live only to the glory of God.

Is that what you desire, dear reader? Have you given your all to God? Is Jesus Christ truly Lord in every area of your life? What about your finances? What about your employment? What about your entertainment? What about your viewing, listening and reading habits? Does anything have mastery over you other than the Lord Jesus Christ? Are you truly living only with an eye to God's glory?

In commenting on the Revelation 4 passage, where John sees the elders falling down and casting their crowns before the throne of God, New Testament scholar William Barclay (1907-1978) notes, "In the ancient world that was the sign of complete submission. When one king surrendered to another, he cast his crown at the victor's feet." Then Barclay adds, "There can be no Christianity without submission."[6] We cannot live to God's glory without living in full surrender and submission to the Lord Jesus Christ.

May our merciful God be able to say of us as Johann von Staupitz (1501-1600) once said to Martin Luther (1483-1546), "It pleases me that the doctrine which you preach ascribes the glory and everything to God alone and nothing to man."[7] Since not many of us are preachers, let's reword that: "It pleases me that the life you live ascribes the glory and everything to God alone and nothing to man."

Is it your desire, dear reader, to live all of your life solely to the glory and honor of our worthy God? If it is, would you now join with me in praying this prayer?

O God, I want your Spirit to perform such a deep work of grace in my heart — and continue performing it — so that I will never again live for my own glory. Forgive me for often robbing you of your deserving glory. Enable me to live for you and you alone. This I offer in the strong name of Jesus. Amen.

CHAPTER 25

The Judgment Seat of Christ

One consuming question that has been at the forefront of my mind now for a good many years is this: *How can I be sure that my works of service will pass the test at the Judgment Seat of Christ?*

Mind you, I'm not *anxious* about my salvation status with our Father in Heaven. With Paul I can say with great assurance, "for I know whom I have believed and I am convinced that He is able to guard what I have entrusted to Him until that day" (1 Tim. 1:12).[1] While I don't take my standing with God for granted, I have the utmost confidence in his ability to preserve me in grace and fellowship and to keep me from falling: "Now to Him who is able to keep you from stumbling, and to make you stand in the presence of His glory blameless with great joy . . ." (Jude 1:24).

But while my standing with God is both a settled fact, the *quality* of service I'm rendering to God is a constant concern. The cry of the sinner is for God's mercy and reconciling salvation. The cry of the Christian is for grace and power to render to the Lord works of service worthy of his name.

The teaching of the inspired apostle in 1 Corinthians 3, clearly addresses this matter of works-quality. Paul takes issue with these spiritually immature Corinthian converts for placing undue importance on the personalities and positions of God's ministering servants. These infants in Christ had developed a personality cult around their favorite minister. As they identified with either Paul or Apollos or Peter, jealousy and quarrels threatened the unity of the church. The gifts and styles of ministry of the three apostles in the eyes of these believers, became more important to them than the Christ each man preached and taught. They were guilty of evaluating a man's ministry by worldly standards instead of leaving it to God to judge a man's work.

It is in this context that Paul assures the Corinthians that the "foundation" that he laid during his ministry among them was the foundation of Jesus Christ (1:11). He then warns (1:12) that every subsequent builder following Paul's ministry—i.e., evangelist and pastor -teacher—needs to take care that he builds with quality teaching and works of service ("gold, silver, precious stones"), and not with inferior materials ("wood, hay, straw"). Next, he makes a sobering claim: "each man's work will become evident; for the day will show it because it is to be revealed with fire, and the fire itself will test the *quality* of each man's work. If any man's work which he has built on it remains, he will receive a reward. If any man's work is burned up, he will suffer loss; but he himself will be saved, yet so as through fire" (vv. 13-15, emphasis added).

Tell me, in light of the above truth, how can any genuine follower and servant of the Lord Jesus Christ be satisfied in *merely* wanting to make it to Heaven? Thank God for his mercy and grace that make Heaven possible for every truly repentant, persevering believer who trusts in the Lamb of God. But will we have anything to lay at the Master's feet once we arrive there? That is what should concern us in the here and now. Will our works of service—Christian service—pass the test of judgment? Will they be burned up, or will they remain? Will we be rewarded, or will we suffer loss? How can I be sure that my works of service will pass the test at the Judgment Seat of Christ? Let us now attempt to provide biblical answers to these questions.

Purified Hearts

No careful student of God's Word can survey the life of the Apostle Peter but what he will note two epochal experiences in this man's life that were life-changing and ministry-transforming. The one was when he laid aside his nets to become a follower of the Lord Jesus Christ; the other was when the Holy Spirit came upon him on the day of Pentecost.

Between Galilee and Pentecost—some three to three and a half years—Simon Peter blew hot and cold in his devotion to his Master and Teacher. He loved Christ, but it was a love mixed with fleshly self-love. He followed Christ, but it was a discipleship of divided loyalties and priorities. One moment he was confessing that Jesus was the Christ, the Son of the living God; and in the next breath he demanded that Jesus avoid the Cross at all costs. At one time he possessed enough faith to walk on water, while on another occasion he didn't possess enough grace to take the lowly place—to be "last," as it were.

At some point in time every earnest disciple of our Lord cries out with Charles Wesley:

Refining fire, go through my heart;
Illuminate my soul;
Scatter Thy life through every part,
And sanctify the whole.[2]

So did Peter. He, along with 119 others, intuitively knew they needed "something more." His double-mindedness was in desperate need of a deep cure. His heart required a radical surgery and wholeness that only his ascended Lord could perform. He had been baptized with water, but he was sorely in need of an inner baptism—a fullness, a fullness of love—the very love of Christ. This, Peter experienced on one glorious day. Suddenly the fiery, purifying presence of the Holy Spirit reached him at his very core, cleansing his ego, filling him with *agape* love. In writing about this years later, the historian Luke records that Peter's heart (along with that of all the other believers in the upper room who were present on the day of Pentecost) was purified on that occasion (Acts 15:8-9).

Without purified hearts our service to Christ will be done with contaminated egos and mixed motives. When works of service are performed with unclean and divided hearts, such service is none other than works of "wood, hay and straw"—works that will not pass the test at the Judgment Seat of Christ.

Why we serve Christ and engage in works of Christian service is fundamentally important. What motivates us to serve as an elder or deacon, witness, give, attend the services of the church, visit the sick, feed the hungry, care for the needy, and a myriad of other good works? Why?

Paul answered this question for himself: "For Christ's love compels us . . ." (2 Cor. 5:14 NIV). And the antecedent experience to this compelling love of Christ is found in "the love of God . . . poured out within our hearts through the Holy Spirit who was given to us" (Rom. 5:5). Is it any wonder that his prayer burden for the Ephesian Christians was that they might "know [personally experience] the love of Christ which surpasses knowledge [human knowledge] . . ." (Eph. 3:19).

None of this means to imply that a Christian receives in one spiritual experience all the divine love he or she will need to meet every contingency of life. We should always be hungering after more and more of Christ's love, being renewed day by day. However, it does suggest that until our hearts have undergone a radical, spiritual circumcision — with all contaminants removed — that we cannot love and serve God and others with sincere and unmixed motives. Only with pure hearts can we build with "gold, silver and precious stones."

Empowered Lives

There is a sense in which heart-purity is power. That is to say, if my will, passions, desires and inclinations have been purified by God's deep cleansing work — and I am experiencing his ongoing work of grace within me — this in itself brings a wholeness and integration to my entire being. The inner conflicts which once dogged my steps, no longer have any power over me, with the very holiness of God taking possession of every compartment of my inner being and transforming all my outer relationships and activities.

But in another sense, one can have a clean temple for the Holy Spirit to dwell in and yet be in need of an ability, a power to *do* the will of God. Pentecost brought these two needs together, meeting their demands. We are in need of pure hearts; we are in need of power to perform works of service and live as overcomers. Pentecost is both purity and power.

If Peter had experienced a pure heart without experiencing a divine anointing and filling, he would have been a good man, living a harmless life, but he would never have stood up fearlessly preaching to the thousands and seen the abundant harvest that he did. Without Holy Spirit power Peter might have been a *sanctified* man but never a *fruitful* man.

On the other hand, if Peter had received God's power without God's purity, he would have been no better than King Saul, who following his departure from God, could still prophesy but not control his temper. Power — even God's power coming through a preacher — may be spectacular and impressive to us, but not to God.

God wants his children to be both sanctified and fruitful instruments of grace. This can only occur as God's people experience the blessing of a personal Pentecost and subsequently live a daily renewed life in the Spirit's power, as they walk in the Spirit so as not to carry out the desires of the flesh (see Gal. 5:16f).

How many of God's children are wanting to do the right and live only for God, but instead go from one defeat to the next? They fail to be consistent overcomers. In their heart of hearts they know they are not living a life that pleases God. Their works of service are done with grudging complaints and grumbles. They have difficulty in resisting temptation. They are often preoccupied with self and appearances. They harbor some unsurrendered area of their hearts and lives. Jesus is not Lord of *all* — not to these believers.

These dear people fill our pulpits and pews. But they're building with wood, hay and straw. They need purity; they need power — Pentecostal purity! Pentecostal power!

Extent and Gifts

The extent of our Christian influence depends upon our respective gifts and callings, and God's sovereign choices for us. Christian works of service done in Jesus' name will take few of us beyond our own localities. But *where* we serve is none of our business. That's God's business. *How* we service is what is fundamental.

Let us be content with where Providence has placed us. Don't aspire to be great. Don't desire to have a wide influence. Aspire to love God with all your heart, soul, mind and strength. Aspire to live a holy, Christlike life. Aspire to be used of God. Aspire to produce a bountiful harvest of fruit to the glory of God that is rich in quality, trusting him to give the increase.

I was recently reading of the far-reaching ministries and lasting fruit of the Twelve Apostles. Here was a small band of unlettered men—blue-collar workers, if you will—who had a life-changing encounter with the Lord Jesus Christ, and who subsequently were purified and empowered by the Holy Spirit. Passionately in love with the Lord Jesus, these men lived daily in the Spirit's power, traveling to the ends of the earth preaching and teaching, healing and building up the body of Christ.

Christian history and tradition informs us that Andrew preached the gospel in Macedonia, Scythia and Russia. Bartholomew preached Christ in many countries, but mostly in India and Armenia. James the Son of Zebedee is believed to be the first Christian missionary to Spain. John's travels took him throughout Asia Minor and the Island of Patmos. Thaddaeus preached in Mesopotamia and Persia. Matthew traveled to Egypt and Ethiopia. Peter evangelized throughout Pontus, Galatia, Bithynia, Cappadocia and Asia. Simon Zelotes preached in Egypt, Mauritania, Africa, Libya and Britain. Thomas' travels took him to India, the Parthians, Medes and Persians. All of these were martyred for their faith with the exception of John, who died a natural death.

On the other hand, there are far more nameless saints who have never engaged in the kind of works of service the apostles did, but who nonetheless have caught God's eye because they are building with gold, silver and precious stones. They are God-purified and Spirit-filled believers. And wherever they live and serve, they are producing quality works to the glory of Christ. Most of these dear people don't stand behind a pulpit or sit on church boards. But their knees are calloused. Their hands are busy. Their feet are worn.

These select saints have a glow in their eye, a song on their lips, and a Presence in their hearts. They live on earth, but dwell in the heavenlies. They enjoy this life, but are living for the next world.

But though these hungry-hearted disciples of Christ are preoccupied with the next world, they go about their Father's business in this world: loving, giving, encouraging, serving, reaching, caring, worshiping, sharing, communing, learning and growing—in the purity and power of the Spirit. Not that they *feel* pure and powerful! These acknowledge more than all the rest their utter dependence upon God and their total reliance upon Christ. They confess that they are helpless sinners apart from the mercy and grace of God, that they are the least of all the saints, that they are totally undeserving of Heaven.

How can we be sure that our works of service will pass the test at the Judgment Seat of Christ? Let us allow God to purify our hearts and cleanse us daily; let us invite the Holy Spirit to empower us and fill us continually. Then let our hope be that when our merciful Lord reviews our life on that Day, that he will find our works of service as gold, silver, and precious stones. Should this be so, let us not think, even now, that we will pass the test because of our own righteousness. Never! It is always grace from beginning to end — God's merciful grace given through the Lord Jesus Christ.

I want to close this chapter with a poem by Martha Snell Nicholson (1898-1953); but before I do, let me share a little about this saintly lady.

Martha was a bedridden invalid for most of her life, who suffered from four incurable diseases. For over thirty-five years, pain was often her daily companion. Though her husband faithfully tended to her needs for many years, he died suddenly, leaving her with added challenges. However, through all of her suffering she wrote some of the very finest Christian poetry. Louis T. Talbot (1889-1976), longtime president of the Bible Institute of Los Angeles (now Biola University), called Martha "one of the most amazing demonstrations of the grace of God that I have witnessed. . . . Out of her troubles were born the exquisite verses which have blessed and comforted thousands of Christians the world around."[3]

While this consecrated lady was confined much of her life to her home in Washington State, her God-glorifying poetry has ministered to God's people around the world for years. What follows is her thoughts on the Judgment Seat of Christ in her own words.

When I stand at the Judgment Seat of Christ
And He shows me His plan for me,
The plan of my life as it might have been,
Had He had His way; and I see
How I blocked Him here, and I checked Him there

And I would not yield my will,
Will there be grief in my Saviour's eyes,
Grief though He loves me still?

He would have me rich, and I stand here poor,
Stripped of all but His grace,
While memory runs like a hunted thing
Down the paths I cannot retrace.
Then my desolate heart will well nigh break
With tears that I cannot shed;
I shall cover my face with my empty hands;
I shall bow my uncrowned head.

Lord of the years that are left to me,
I give them to Thy hand;
Take me and break me, mold me to
The pattern Thou hast planned.[4]

I pray that in that Day, my works will not be seen by my Lord to be as "wood, hay, straw," but as "gold, silver, precious stones" — fruit that will pass his approving inspection. If that should be my lot, it will all be because of his merciful grace alone toward this unworthy sinner saved by his grace. "For we must all appear before the judgment seat of Christ, so that each one may be recompensed for his deeds in the body, according to what he has done, whether good or bad" (2 Cor. 5:10).

Endnotes

Introduction
1. Retrieved from http://lovechapelhill.wordpress.com/page/64/?
    ref=spelling.

Chapter 1: Christ *in* You
1. Unless otherwise noted, all Bible references in this chapter are taken
    from the *The Holy Bible, New International Version.*
2. Samuel Chadwick, *The Way to Pentecost* (Berne, IN: Light and Hope Pub-
    lications, 1937), 15.
3. Joe Brice, *Pentecost* (London: Hodder & Stoughton, 1936, reprinted by
    Convention Book Store, 1973), 25-26.

Chapter 2: Grace and Salvation (Part 1)
1. Unless otherwise noted, all Bible quotations in this chapter are taken
    from *The Holy Bible, English Standard Version.*
2. This account has been used with the kind permission of Dr. John D. Ab-
    bott, Jr.
3. Taken from "And Can It Be?" by Charles Wesley.
4. A. W. Tozer, *The Knowledge of the Holy* (New York: Harper & Brothers,
    1961), 88.
5. Taken from "Jesus, the Very Thought of Thee" by Bernard of Clairvaux.
6. Wesley, Ibid.

Chapter 3: Grace and Salvation (Part 2)
1. Unless otherwise noted, all Bible references in this chapter are taken
    from *The Holy Bible, English Standard Version.*
2. C. S. Lewis, *Surprised by Joy* (New York: Harcourt Brace Jovanovich Pub-
    lishers, 1955), 228, 237.
3. C. S. Lewis, *Mere Christianity*, revised (New York: MacMillan Publishing
    Co., 1952), 182.
4. Taken from "Startled Beyond Measure: How D. James Kennedy Came to

Christ." Retrieved from www.truthinaction.org.
5. Taken from "At Calvary" by William R. Newell.
6. Taken from "There's a Wideness in God's Mercy" by Frederick W. Faber.
7. Ibid., *Mere Christianity*, 140.
8. Charles W. Colson, *Born Again* (Old Tappan, NJ: Revell, 1976), 130.
9. Taken from "I Was a Wandering Sheep" by Horatius Bonar.

Chapter 4: Total Consecration (Part 1)
1. Murray J. Harris, *Slave for Christ* (Downers Grove, IL: InterVarsity Press, 1999), 18.
2. These words are variously rendered in English versions of the Bible. For example, in the NT the Greek word *hagiazō* is translated by the ESV as *sanctify, make holy, consecrated*, etc.
3. Unless otherwise noted, all Bible references in this chapter are taken from *The Holy Bible, English Standard Version*.
4. Frederick W. Danker, *A Greek-English Lexicon of the New Testament and Other Early Christian Literature*, rev. and ed., 3rd. ed. [CD-ROM]. Based on Walter Bauer's Griechisch-deutsches Wörterbuch zu den Scriften des Neuen Testaments under früh-christlichen Literatur, sixth edition, ed. Kurt Aland and Barbara Aland, with Viktor Reichmann and on previous English editions by W. F. Arndt, F. W. Gingrich, and F. W. Danker (BDAG), (Chicago: University of Chicago Press, 2000), 10.
5. Taken from "Take My Life and Let It Be" by Frances Havergal.
6. For example, his deceptions in Genesis 12:10-20 and Genesis 20:1-18.
7. G. Steinberger, *In the Footsteps of the Lamb*, (Minneapolis: Bethany House Publishers, 2000, reprinted from 1936), 46.
8. Frederick Dale Bruner, *Matthew, A Commentary*, vol. 2, rev. ed. (Grand Rapids: William B. Eerdmans Publishing Co., 1990), 149.
9. Dietrich Bonhoeffer, *Discipleship, Dietrich Bonhoeffer Works*, Vol. 4, translated from the German edition edited by Martin Kuske and Ilse Tödt; English edition edited by Geffrey B. Kelly and John D. Godsey; translated by Barbara Green and Richard Krauss (Minneapolis: Fortress Press, 2003), 85.
10. Ibid., 91.
11. François Fénelon, *Talking With God*, Modern English version by Hal M. Helms (Brewster, MA: Paraclete Press, 1997), 103.

Chapter 5: Total Consecration (Part 2)
1. Unless otherwise noted, all Bible references in this chapter are taken from *The Holy Bible, English Standard Version*.
2. Romans 1:13; 7:1, 4; 8:12; 10:1; 11:25; 12:1; 15:14; 15:30; 16:17.
3. Joseph H. Fitzmyer, *Romans: A New Translation with Introduction and Commentary, The Anchor Bible*, Vol. 33 (New York: Doubleday, 1993), 249.
4. Jean-Pierre de Caussade, *The Joy of Full Surrender*, rev. trans. by Hal M. Helms of *L'Abandon à la Providence Divine* (Brewster, MA: Paraclete

Press, 1986), 70.

5. John R. W. Stott, *The Message of Romans* (Downers Grove, IL: InterVarsity Press, 1994), 321.

6. C. F. D. Moule, *An Idiom Book of New Testament Greek* (Cambridge: University Press, 1968), 10.

7. Fritz Rienecker, *A Linguistic Key to the Greek New Testament*. Cleon L. Rogers, Jr., ed. (Grand Rapids: Zondervan Publishing House, 1976),

8. Fitzmyer, 639.

9. Thomas C. Oden, *Life in the Spirit, Systematic Theology*, vol. 3 (New York: HarperCollins Publishers, 1992), 401.

10. Matthew Henry, *Matthew Henry's Commentary on the Whole Bible*, vol. VI (Old Tappan, NJ: Fleming H. Revell Co., n. d.), 455.

11. H. C. G. Moule, *The Epistle to the Romans*, Philip Hillyer, ed. (Fort Washington, PA: CLC Publications, 1958), 260.

12. See, for example, 1 Thessalonians 5:23 where Paul uses "your whole spirit and soul and body" with reference to God's sanctifying work.

13. See, for example, 1 Corinthians 1:2: "to those sanctified in Christ Jesus."

14. John Murray, *The Epistle to the Romans* (Grand Rapids: William B. Eerdmans Publishing Co., 1965), 149.

15. Taken from "All for Jesus" by Mary D. James.

Chapter 6: The Pure in Heart (Part 1)

1. Unless otherwise noted, all Bible references in this chapter are taken from *The Holy Bible, English Standard Version*.

2. See Hebrews 11:22; Acts 15:9.

3. Frederick Dale Bruner, *Matthew, A Commentary*, vol. 1, rev. ed. (Grand Rapids: William B. Eerdmans Publishing Co., 2004), 175.

4. W. E. Sangster, *The Path to Perfection* (New York: Abingdon-Cokesbury, 1943), 135.

5. Retrieved from http://www.sermonindex.net/modules/articles/index.php?view=article&aid=10393.

6. Andrew Bonar, *Robert Murray M'Cheyne* (London: The Banner of Truth Trust, 1962, reprint), 185.

Chapter 7: The Pure in Heart (Part 2)

1. Unless otherwise noted, all Bible references in this chapter are taken from *The Holy Bible, English Standard Version*.

2. A. J. Gordon, *The Ministry of the Spirit* (Philadelphia: American Baptist Publication Society, 1896), 116-117.

3. A. B. Simpson, *The Holy Spirit: Power from on High*, Keith M. Bailey, ed. (Camp Hill, PA: Christian Publications, 1994), 374.

4. Samuel Chadwick, *The Way to Pentecost* (Berne, IN: Light & Hope Publications, 1937), 15.

5. Ibid., 17.

Chapter 8: The Pure in Heart (Part 3)
1. Unless otherwise noted, all Bible references in this chapter are taken from *The Holy Bible, English Standard Version.*
2. E. Stanley Jones, *A Song of Ascents: A Spiritual Autobiography,* (Nashville: Abingdon, 1968), 34.

Chapter 9: The Pure in Heart (Part 4)
1. Unless otherwise noted, all Bible references in this chapter are taken from *The Holy Bible, English Standard Version.*
2. F. F. Bruce, *The Epistle to the Hebrews,* p. 202.
3. Taken from "Not All the Blood of Beasts" by Isaac Watts.
4. Ibid.

Chapter 10: The Crucified Life
1. Unless otherwise noted, all Bible references in this chapter are taken from *The Holy Bible, English Standard Version.*

Chapter 11: The Risen Life
1. Unless otherwise noted, all Bible references in this chapter are taken from *The Holy Bible, English Standard Version.*
2. Taken from "Rescue the Perishing" by Fanny Crosby.
3. William Barclay, *Flesh and Spirit* (Grand Rapids: Baker, 1976), 113.
4. Taken from "Lord Jesus, Make Thyself to Me" by Charlotte Elliott.

Chapter 12: Wounded by God
1. Unless otherwise noted, all Bible references in this chapter are taken from *The Holy Bible, New International Version.*
2. According to my research, Angela Morgan is the author of the original poem titled "When Nature Wants a Man." It was possibly Henry F. Lyte who altered Morgan's poem, creating this often quoted verse.
3. Lettie Cowman, *Springs in the Valley* (Los Angeles: The Oriental Missionary Society, 1939), 62.

Chapter 13: From Gold to God
1. Douglas Hanks, Jr., ***Driven by the Stars: The Story of Durward Knowles*** by Douglas Hanks, Jr.; (self-published, 1992), 120. I am indebted to Mr. Hanks for some background material for this article as well. He kindly gave his permission for the quotes I used from his excellent biography.
2. Ibid. 138-139.
3. Ibid., 149.
4. Ibid., 189.

Chapter 14: When God Comes Near (Part 1)
1. Unless otherwise noted, all Bible references in this chapter are taken from *The Holy Bible, English Standard Version.*

2.   John Owen, *Introduction* by J. I. Packer in *Triumph over Temptation*, James M. Houston, ed. (Colorado Springs, CO: Cook Communications, 2005), 21
3.   See Psalm 51.
4.   David Wilkerson, "Times Square Church Pulpit Series," August 2, 1999.

Chapter 15: When God Comes Near (Part 2)
1.   Unless otherwise noted, all Bible references in this chapter are taken from *The Holy Bible, English Standard Version*.
2.   E. Stanley Jones, *A Song of Ascents* (Nashville: Abingdon Press, 1968), 34-35.

Chapter 16: A Praying Prophet
1.   Unless otherwise noted, all Bible references in this chapter are taken from the *New American Standard Bible*.
2.   See 1 Samuel 3:1-14.
3.   A. W. Tozer, *The Praying Plumber of Lisburn* (Harrisburg, PA: Christian Publications, n. d.), 24.

Chapter 17: The "Ifs" of Jesus
1.   Unless otherwise noted, all Bible references in this chapter are taken from *The Holy Bible, English Standard Version*.
2.   Dietrich Bonhoeffer, *The Cost of Discipleship* (New York: Macmillan, 1966), 53, emphasis added.
3.   Literal translation.
4.   Eugene H. Peterson, *A Long Obedience in the Same Direction* (Downers Grove, IL: InterVarsity Press, 1980), 13. (Peterson borrowed this saying from Friedrich Nietzsche and *sanctified* it!)

Chapter 18: The Apollos Problem
1.   I fully realize the text is not explicit in what is meant in Acts 18:26 by "But when Priscilla and Aquila heard him, they took him aside and ex-plained the to him the way of God *more accurately*." However, when one considers that Apollos "was mighty in the Scriptures (18:24); that he "had been instructed in the way of the Lord" (18:25); that he "was speak-ing and teaching the things concerning Jesus" (18:25); that he was "acquainted only with the baptism of John" (18:25); and that in Acts 18 the Ephesian disciples "had never heard whether there is a Holy Spir-it" (19:2), having only experienced "John's baptism" (19:2) before being filled with the Holy Spirit under Paul's teaching — it is a logical deduc-tion, in my view, that *what* Priscilla and Aquila discerned that Apollos lacked was the *power* that results from being "clothed with power from on high" (Luke 24:49).
2.   William Barclay, *The Acts of the Apostles f the Apostles, The Daily Study Bible Series*, rev. ed. (Philadelphia: The Westminster Press, 1976), 139.

3. Ibid.
4. Unless otherwise noted, all Bible references in this chapter are taken from the *New American Standard Bible.*
5. Samuel Chadwick, *The Way to Pentecost* (Berne, IN: Light and Hope Publications, 1937), 15-16.
5. Martyn Lloyd-Jones, *Joy Unspeakable* (Wheaton, IL: Harold Shaw Publishers, 1985), 114.
6. Ibid., 113-114.
7. George and Donald Sweeting, *Lessons from the Life of Moody*, revised (Chicago: Moody Press, 2001), 96-97.

Chapter 19: Living a Focused Life
1. Unless otherwise noted, all Bible references in this chapter are taken from *The Holy Bible, English Standard Version.*
2. Thomas Kelly, *A Testament of Devotion* (New York: Harper & Brothers,, 1941), 80.
3. Os Guinness, *The Call* (Nashville: Word, 2003), 164-166.
4. "Christian History" (Worchester, PA: Christian History Institute), 80:3.
5. Quoted in *On the Father Front* by Ray Pritchard, Vol. 8, No. 2, 1995.

Chapter 20: Reflecting Christ's Image
1. Unless otherwise noted, all Bible references in this chapter are taken from *The Holy Bible, English Standard Version.*
2. Taken from "I Want to Be Like Jesus" by Thomas O. Chisholm.

Chapter 21: Why Pastors Weep
1. Taken from "Rescue the Perishing" by Fanny Crosby.
2. Leonard Ravenhill, "Weeping Between the Porch and the Altar." Retrieved from http://www.ravenhill.org/weeping1.htm.

Chapter 22: Power and Authority in the Church
1. A. W. Tozer, *God Tells the Man Who Cares* (Harrisburg, PA: Christian Publications, 1970), 166-172.
2. Eugene Peterson, *The Message: The New Testament in Contemporary English* (Colorado Springs, CO: NavPress, 1993), 368.

Chapter 23: To God Be the Glory
1. Unless otherwise noted, all Bible references in this chapter are taken from the *The Holy Bible, New International Version.*
2. Dennis F. Kinlaw, *Preaching in the Spirit* (Grand Rapids: Zondervan, 1985), 46.
3. George Whitefield, *George Whitefield's Journals* (Carlisle, PA: The Banner of Truth Trust, reprint 1998), Nov. 29, 1739.
4. Cited by Timothy George in "Delighted by Doctrine." Retrieved from http://www.beesondivinity.com/delightedbydoctrine.

Chapter 24: Living to the Glory of God

1. All Scripture references are taken from the *New American Standard Bible* except as noted.
2. Reuben A (Bud) Robinson, *My Life's Story* (Kansas City: Nazarene Publishing House, 1928). Retrieved from wesley.nnu.edu.
3. Taken from "Take My Life and Let It Be" by Frances R. Havergal.
4. J. Gilchrist Lawson, *Deeper Experiences of Famous Christians* (Anderson, IN: Warner Press, 1911), 313.
5. A. W. Tozer, The *Pursuit of God* (Harrisburg, PA: Christian Publications, 1948), 127.
6. William Barclay, *The Revelation of John, Daily Bible Studies Series,* vol. 1, rev. ed. (Philadelphia: The Westminster Press, 1976), 163-64.
7. Cited by John Piper, *The Legacy of Sovereign Joy* (Wheaton, IL: Crossway Books, 2000), 24.

Chapter 25: The Judgment Seat of Christ

1. Unless otherwise noted, all Bible references in this chapter are taken from the *New American Standard Bible.*
2. Taken from "Jesus, Thine All-Victorious Love" by Charles Wesley.
3. Retrieved from http://www.pulpithelps.com/www/docs/1128-8649.
4. Retrieved from http://www.cavaliersonly.com poetry_by_christian_ poets_of_the_past/poetry_by_martha_snell_nicholson.

More books by Ralph I. Tilley

Thirsting for God

Letters from Noah
(historical fiction)

The Mind of Christ by John R. MacDuff
(edited reprint)

A Passion for Christ

*How Christ Came to Church: An Anthology of the Works of
A. J. Gordon*
(edited reprint)

Breath of God

The Christian's Vital Breath

Not Peace But a Sword by Vance Havner
Introduction by Ralph I. Tilley
(fiction reprint)

Christ in You

The Bow in the Cloud by John R. MacDuff
(edited reprint)

Books available at either . . .

litsjournal.org
amazon.com